"Vicki Caruana has written a book that will assist every parent who asks the question: 'How can I be the best advocate for my child?' Whether you have been a buddy, a bully, or a hero when your son or daughter needed help, you will learn techniques in Standing Up for Your Child that will give you hands-on tools to support your offspring in an appropriate way that promotes positive action and a favorable result. Every parent of school-age children should read this book!"

—CAROL KENT, speaker and author
A New Kind of Normal (Thomas Nelson)

"When it comes to standing up for your child, are you a steamroller—or sitting it out? I've seen both extremes, and so has Vicki Caruana. In this book, she shows you how to avoid the mistakes so many parents make in the classroom, on the playing field, and in the doctor's office. If you champion your child Vicki's way, he or she will have good reason to thank you—and so will those teachers, coaches, and pediatricians."

—RUTH A. PETERS, PH.D.
Clinical psychologist, author, and
contributor to NBC's *Today* show

"No other human knows and cares about your child as much as you do. So when he or she faces bullying at school, benchwarming on the soccer field, or misdiagnosis at the clinic, it's no wonder you feel like going on the warpath. But too many parents let their anger overwhelm them—or 'the system' intimidate them. This book will help you understand how the process really works—and how it can work for the benefit of everyone involved."

—JIM BURNS, PH.D.
President, HomeWord

"Raising children in today's world is, for a thoughtful Christian, a challenge of the first order. Any parent would be well served to follow Vicki Caruana's survey of our cultural battlefield and the parent's place in that war zone. For the Christian parent, coming to grips with the need to be prepared is imperative, and Vicki's helpful guide provides welcome insights into the self-evaluation process that will stiffen your resolve and help you be an effective parent when Standing Up for Your Child."

—PAUL PETERSEN, president
A Minor Consideration

"As a member of the U.S. Olympic team, I'm amazed how much we as parents need to be effective advocates for our children whether it be with teachers, coaches, spouses, or before the child is born. Every parent needs this book to show them how to do this with integrity, honor, and conviction. Learn how to be your child's hero and protect them while keeping your character. It's a wonderful book."

—TRISH PORTER
1988 U.S. Olympian
World record holder, age 40-44, high jump

Standing Up for Your Child
without Stepping on Toes

FOCUS ON THE FAMILY

STANDING UP
FOR YOUR CHILD
without stepping on toes

Vicki Caruana

TYNDALE HOUSE PUBLISHERS, INC.

CAROL STREAM, ILLINOIS

Cover design by Erik M. Petersen
Cover photograph by Image Source/JupiterImages. All rights reserved.

Library of Congress Cataloging-in-Publication Data
Caruana, Vicki.
  Standing up for your child without stepping on toes / Vicki Caruana.
     p. cm.
  ISBN-13: 978-1-58997-365-7
  ISBN-10: 1-58997-365-8
  1. Parenting—Religious aspects—Christianity. 2. Helping behavior—Religious aspects—Christianity. I. Title.
  BV4529.C428 2007
  248.8'45—dc22
                                    2006101648

Printed in the United States of America
1 2 3 4 5 6 7 8 9 / 12 11 10 09 08 07

To the real-life advocates in my life—Jenny, Steve, Tony, Hilda, Carrie, and Terry. Thank you for standing up for my needs throughout my career.

CONTENTS

ACKNOWLEDGMENTS

I am so grateful for all those parents who shared their stories with me as selfless contributors to this book. In part these contributions were used to further research for my doctoral work as well. Parents from all over the U.S. shared their fears, frustrations, failures, and fleeting successes with advocacy. I specifically want to thank those who participated in my online parent survey for taking precious time away from their families to do so.

I also want to thank Marita Littauer for spreading the word through her networks that I needed parent contributions. Her support means so much to me. Thanks also to the women of AWSA, the Advanced Writers and Speakers Association, who took a moment out of their busy writing lives to share with me how they stand up for their children.

Finally, I want to thank my husband, Chip, who argued with me more than once about what standing up for your children really means.

This is a stronger book because of all those who shared their family stories with me.

INTRODUCTION

W hat do you want for your children?

You want the best for them. You want quality experiences with quality people. You want them to be happy and healthy. You want them to be successful and lead productive, satisfying lives. At the same time, you want to protect them, prepare them, and prevent them from making mistakes.

All this is natural and normal. But just wanting something may not get you what you're looking for.

Sometimes you have to take action. Sometimes you find yourself in a battle zone for the sake of your child. Sometimes people get hurt in the process.

It's been suggested to me that it's not possible to stand up for your child without stepping on toes. I disagree. If we're careful about how we communicate and conduct ourselves, we can help our children get what we think they need in a way that doesn't burn bridges, alienate, or betray our claims to be followers of Christ.

There will be obstacles in your way. There will be people and circumstances you can control and those you can't. There will be disappointments and discouragements. Yet this is a road that faith-filled parents should be prepared to walk with their children.

There are internal obstacles, too. Our personalities, experiences, and abilities can get in the way of our desire to provide our children with what they want or need.

My mother used to say I was my own worst enemy—that I got in my own way. She was right. Now, as a parent, I want to do better than I did for myself. I don't want to discover that I'm the one who got in my children's way.

That happens to many of us, and more often than you might think. We spend so much time doing damage control, negotiating, going to bat for, and otherwise standing up for our kids that we don't focus on what's really important.

Eventually our children need to learn to stand up for themselves, and the sooner the better. Throughout this book you'll discover not only what it takes to stand up for your kids without stepping on toes, but to train them in being their own champions.

There are hundreds, maybe thousands, of scenarios that require parental intervention; there's no way I could cover every situation. Instead, I offer you guiding principles, along with examples from the lives of those who contributed to this book, in a way that helps you apply what you learn to your life with your children.

Speaking of anecdotes, the ones you're about to read are a mix of real-life, based-on-real-life, and composite stories. Names have been changed to protect the identities of parents and their children. Gleaned from an online parent survey, from fellow members of various groups and organizations, and from my circle of friends, these stories offer examples of what it takes to stand up for your child in today's world.

How to Use This Book

First, take a deep breath. You're about to be submerged in a world you thought you knew.

Standing up for your child is not a mystery. It's something you do instinctively. But the mother- or father-bear behavior that surfaces when your child is threatened must be tamed if you're going to accomplish anything. This book is a guide to doing that.

It's not a bible, though. It's full of proverbial wisdom, not a to-do checklist. I suggest reading it all the way through, deferring judgment until you reach the end. There is an actual method behind the madness amidst these pages.

After your first read-through, focus on one principle that you believe speaks to your current situation. Ask God to show you any hard-heartedness you harbor, and to soften you toward His will for you and your child. Consider your accountability to Him and the reputation you present to a watching world.

> The mother- or father-bear behavior that surfaces when your child is threatened must be tamed if you're going to accomplish anything.

Finally, give yourself and your child a break. Guess what? Your son or daughter isn't perfect, and neither are you. You'll make mistakes when you stand up; your child will make mistakes when standing up for himself or herself. You're both in the process of becoming.

The fields of communication, psychology, business, and even evangelism all have something to teach us about advocacy. The topic easily can become controversial, too; emotions run high when we talk about our children's rights, needs, and desires.

That's why I've created a place where you can meet with other parents just like you who need support as they stand up for their children. Please visit us at www.standingupforyour child.blogspot.com.

1

IN THE BEGINNING

S ometimes standing up for your child starts when he or she is still in the womb.

For us, it began after losing our first child, Emily, to an unusual genetic disorder.

During the sixteenth week of both of my subsequent pregnancies, in 1989 and 1991 respectively, I had to decide whether to undergo amniocentesis to find out whether these babies, like the first, had Turner's syndrome. The procedure included penetrating my abdomen with a terrifyingly long needle, in search of amniotic fluid that would be analyzed. Since I was classified as "high risk," the doctor insisted the test was necessary.

Not that it mattered. My husband, Chip, and I agreed long before the procedure that even if the results revealed that this child too had Turner's Syndrome, we would see the pregnancy through to term, God willing.

After the first time I underwent this probing—almost alien—procedure, we were referred to a genetic counselor.

It was just six months since our daughter had died before her first breath. We hadn't possessed the experience, wisdom, or the opportunity to stand up for Emily's chance at life. That chance had been statistically nonexistent; we knew she was dying in utero and couldn't do anything to stop it.

Now the counselor, Pam, sat facing us. She extended her right hand to me and her left to my husband. "I'm your bridge," she said. "We have a lot to talk about, but first things first."

Who would stand in the gap for our baby? We would.

Sitting on the edge of the hard plastic chair, I breathed a sigh of relief. Finally, I thought, we'd found someone who could understand the agony Chip and I had been through. We wouldn't have to explain and explain again the depth of our pain and confusion at the loss of Emily.

In Pam, we had someone who'd stand up for our choice—even against doctors who proposed something else. We'd never had that before. We'd been alone, feeling pressure from well-meaning experts. Pam had seen it all and worked with countless other parents who struggled with genetic uncertainties. She could speak the language of the medical community and translate when necessary.

Squeezing my hand, Chip smiled at me with his own sense of relief. We were going to be okay.

Or so we thought.

"Before I can advocate for you as parents, I need to make sure I understand your wishes," Pam began. "This time, if the fetus presents with the same chromosomal defect, would you prefer to terminate instead of waiting for the inevitable death in utero? There's no reason to put yourself through that pain again."

Any relief I'd felt dissipated like cheap air freshener. Pam was really one of *them*.

She'd said she was there to advocate for our wishes, but she'd made assumptions about what those wishes were. Termination was not a choice in our minds. It seemed that, once again, we were alone in standing up for our child.

Once again I was bargaining with someone who didn't share my beliefs or convictions. Pam was kind, professional, and knowledgeable, but she didn't get it. Even as she tried to soothe our raw emotions, I realized she couldn't possibly be the advocate we needed.

Chip released Pam's hand and squeezed mine tighter.

"We're ready this time, no matter what the test shows," he said.

Who would stand in the gap for our baby? We would. It was what we'd been called to do from the moment of his conception.

This was the day we started to learn what it meant to advocate for our children. This was the beginning of the goofy, gratifying, challenge-riddled time of our lives called parenthood.

We would learn that, for better and for worse, in sickness and in health, in school and on the playground, at grandma's house and on the soccer field, in the dentist's chair and beyond, parents question and quarrel and sometimes quiver or quit when faced with something that threatens their children's quality of life.

Sometimes they're blessed with someone to stand beside them when they stand up for their children. More often they stand alone—or so it seems.

As for our firstborn son, Christopher—he did not have Turner's Syndrome. Nor did his brother, Charles.

So with two boys to raise, it was time for the long-term work of advocacy to begin.

Standing Up and Standing Down

Think back to when you were growing up. Most likely you experienced at least one situation in which you had to stand up for someone else.

Maybe you stood up for your brother against a bully. Maybe you stood up for your best friend against a hurtful rumor. Maybe you stood up for yourself against your parents' demand for an unreasonable curfew. Whatever the reason, you felt compelled to open your mouth in response to some injustice, misunderstanding, or mistreatment.

Chances are that you were and continue to be one of the good guys. As a parent you probably stand up, stand firm, and at times stand against injustice—whether it's directed at your child or someone else's.

Some of us, though, do more than stand up for the rights of the weak. We may be guilty of shoving our way down the throats of others, even if our cause has merit. We're the parents who make the news, caught on the school security camera as we climb over the front counter in the office and throttle the assistant principal. We're the parents who scream at coaches through the metal fences near the bleachers in order to "encourage" them to give our children more game time.

As severe as this sounds, it happens too often. Parents behaving badly give nightmares to teachers, coaches, doctors, nurses, and other service providers. Those of us who pose for this not-so-pretty picture are *bully parents*.

On the other hand, perhaps you've been faced with injustice and did nothing. You may have stood by while a bully picked on a less-than-popular kid at school. You may have let a friend repeat a lie about a classmate when you knew it wasn't true. You may have sat quietly in the bleachers when a coach screamed your child into the ground about an error he made.

Has inaction defined you? Do you struggle to stand tall against the giants who tower over you and your child's life? Those of us who whimper and wilt at the thought of confrontation are *victim parents*.

I've described the extremes here. But we all have a tendency toward one or the other.

Which way do you naturally bend? Trees grow toward the sun, twisting and turning around obstacles as they do. You can tell the trees that usually face a fierce wind; their trunks and branches curl away from it. We either grow in response to something that satisfies us or against something that threatens us. And so do our children.

We're the parents who scream at coaches through the metal fences near the bleachers in order to "encourage" them to give our children more game time.

Worse Than Ever?

Some say parents need to pay more attention than ever to the issue of advocacy. Consider the following, adapted from a column I wrote in response to an Associated Press article about a parent who stormed into her daughter's classroom unannounced.

School Violence Hits an All-time Low

What happens when two mother bears fight over the same cub? Well, one gets jailed and the other ends up in the emergency room. On October 22, 2004 in Macon, Georgia, a teacher was charged with battery and cruelty to children for allegedly beating a parent who tried to retrieve her daughter's backpack.

Talk about violence in schools!

Both parents and teachers are territorial when it comes to children in school.

"This is my room. These are my kids," a teacher declares.

"This is my family. These are my kids," a parent defends.

Both play the role of protector and defender of their own territories—and children get caught in the middle.

There's a good chance the parent didn't follow proper procedures and walked into the teacher's classroom both uninvited and unexpected. There's an even better chance that there was a history of negative encounters between this parent and teacher. Most likely, both parties had personal issues outside of school that affected their aberrant behavior that day.

The tug-of-war over the student's backpack was inappropriate at worst and childish at best. When the teacher threw the backpack in the trash, it was perceived as a declaration of war. A struggle ensued, hair was pulled, punches were thrown—and finally the teacher picked up a chair and hit the mom on the back.

All while the children watched.

Parents worry quite a bit about violence in schools. I doubt any of us thought that it was the teachers we had to be afraid of.

"Cruelty to children" was one of the charges against

that teacher. I commend the court that made that charge. It keeps the focus where it should be—on the children.

Not only should grown-ups know better, but the bottom line is that it is not about us! We've already had our turn. This is our children's one shot at a quality education. Without real parent-teacher partnerships, our kids will get the raw end of the deal. But without mutual respect there will be no partnerships.

We can't just assume that everyone involved in a child's life is there for the same purpose. We need to take the time to get to know those adults who sometimes spend more time with our kids than we do. Partnerships don't just happen. They require time, attention, and the dismantling of fences.

We must do all this and more. Parents need to respect an authority figure's position and boundaries. Authorities must re-spect a parent's position and values. Both can talk together kindly, plan together wisely, and support one another regularly.

All while the children watch.

Whether or not the advocacy battle is more intense than ever, it feels that way sometimes.

I've certainly felt like a mother bear protecting her cub on more than one occasion—though sometimes I'm not nearly as ferocious as I think I should be. I have this habit of expecting other people to be on their best behavior, but usually I'm disappointed to discover that they're not.

One day, for instance, I sat on a bench at the playground and watched as a seven-year-old girl pushed my four-year-old son off the steps to what we called "the big climbing toy." She dismissed him as if swatting a fly.

Standing, I took one step forward—hoping my grown-up presence would fill the girl's view and dissuade her from pushing my son again. He clambered up the sturdy steps one more time; again she pushed back.

This time I stood where the little darling's mother could see me, spotting my son with both hands as he climbed up the steps. When the girl reached out to push him down, I blocked her maneuver. "No. Keep your hands in your own space," my teacher voice said. "It's his turn to climb."

She screamed.

Guess what? Her mother tore herself away from her phone conversation and yelled at me to leave her daughter alone.

Me! She yelled at *me*!

Toe to toe we stood, my sneakers firmly planted and her three-inch heels sinking into the newly spread mulch. Then, nose to nose with her, I felt my resolve begin to dissipate.

My insides shuddered as they do when my blood sugar plummets. I stood and said, "I would appreciate it if we could play on the big climbing toy, too. Everyone deserves a turn."

For a moment she said nothing, eyeing me like a cat ready to pounce on an unsuspecting bird. Suddenly she turned, yanked her daughter off the big climbing toy, and dragged her, screaming, to their SUV.

I felt weak in the knees for a moment. Then I turned to see my son atop the big climbing toy, a smile stretching from ear to ear.

Everybody Needs One

We all need an advocate—someone to stand up for us, at least until we can stand on our own.

Most of us have had such a champion. Maybe your parents were your first advocates, and as you grew you encountered others who stood in the gap for you. Many people apparently long to be heroes, looking for ways to save someone or something else. Teachers, coaches, friends, family, and even strangers speak for those who don't have a voice of their own. There are whole organizations devoted to advocacy—for children, endangered species, the environment, the needy, the persecuted, the homeless, the misunderstood, and the wrongly accused.

We parents are charged with being advocates for our children. From the moment they're conceived, we make decisions about their quality of life. Our choices don't always mirror those encouraged by our doctors, families, and friends—which is why standing up for our kids risks stepping on toes.

Take, for example, the choice of how to deliver your baby. Did you go all-natural or medicated? Did you enroll in Lamaze, Bradley, or no childbirth class? What did you say when your doctor asked if you were going to breast-feed or bottle-feed your newborn? If you had a son, how did you decide whether or not to circumcise him? These were all opportunities to stand up for the needs of your child and the rest of your family. It was the beginning of a lifelong commitment—and perhaps some lifelong disagreements.

There are times when parents need advocates, too—someone to help when we have trouble getting our children what they need. Sometimes an issue is too big for us to handle on our own; sometimes we just don't know how to get answers.

Knowing how to choose an advocate and acting as one yourself often require the same skill set. In the following chapters you'll discover guiding principles that will help you develop and exercise those skills—in a way that makes your advocacy effective and consistent with your values.

Ready or Not, Stand Up

I certainly wasn't prepared to advocate for the life of our preborn son all those years ago. But I was thrust into the role anyway.

Maybe you anticipate a big "fight" on the horizon on behalf of your child, and you hope this book will help prepare you for it. Maybe your child has a chronic or life-threatening illness that forced you into this role early on. Whether it's due to a mental, physical, relational, or spiritual cause, you may always find yourself on call to stand in the gap—ready or not.

Does your child have a learning disability? Is she gifted? A benchwarmer? A prodigy? Do you find yourself having to defend your child to another son or daughter or even your own spouse? Does living in a blended, single, or extended family complicate the problem? What if a friend allows your child to watch television shows and movies that you don't allow in your home? Are you battling humanism in a public school, legalism in a private Christian school, or competitive philosophies if you homeschool? Is your child learning how to stand up for herself by watching you?

Whether advocating for your child shoots tingles of intimidation or exhilaration down your spine, you won't lack for opportunities. Let this book help you hone your "stand-up" skills—so that when the time comes, you can be your child's hero.

2

THE PERFECT ADVOCATE

When it comes to standing up for your child, who makes the best role model? Do you want to imitate the mom who fought the teacher over the backpack? A favorite uncle who talked the tennis coach into letting you join the varsity team?

How about Someone who's perfect?

Consider the example of God Himself. You may be familiar with the biblical concept that He exists as three persons—Father, Son, and Holy Spirit. But have you thought about what a great advocate He is?

1. *Jesus stands in our place.* An advocate pleads the cause of another. Even while dying on the cross, Jesus did that for us when He said, "Father, forgive them; for they do not know what they are doing" (Luke 23:34).

He's still doing that today. "Who is the one who condemns?

Christ Jesus is He who died, yes, rather who was raised, who is at the right hand of God, who also intercedes for us" (Romans 8:34).

Jesus stands before a holy God, so that when God the Father looks at us He doesn't see our sin. He sees His Son, if we've placed our faith in Him. Jesus is our bridge to God the Father: "I am the way, and the truth, and the life; no one comes to the Father but through Me" (John 14:6).

What can we learn from the way Jesus advocates for us?

- He doesn't hesitate to put Himself in harm's way for our sakes. He not only says He'd take my place; He actually does it.
- He doesn't balk at associating with people who are less than perfect, people who need Him to be their champion.
- His reputation, His good name, paves the way for us.
- His actions are selfless; His love, unwavering.

Why does Jesus stand up for me before His Father? Why does He sacrifice even His life for me, a wayward child who has yet to understand the consequences of her actions?

The answer: love. "But God demonstrates His own love toward us, in that while we were yet sinners, Christ died for us" (Romans 5:8).

Am I willing to do the same for my children? Is my love for them strong enough that I'll advocate for their needs as Jesus does for mine?

2. The Holy Spirit steps in so we can understand and be understood. There are times when we just don't understand what's being said. Sometimes we need an interpreter when the culture or language is foreign to us. We need someone to explain what the words mean.

Our genetic counselor, Pam, was supposed to be that person for my husband and me. She was well versed in the language of doctors and knew how to explain things in a way we would understand. But there was one glitch in her translation. She didn't attach the same value to the message that we did; her interpretation was biased.

One reason the Holy Spirit came was to open the Bible to us in a way we could understand. What at first glance might look like gibberish becomes meaningful. The Spirit not only understands the message, but knows intimately the hearts of both the sender and receiver. As one Bible translation puts it, "But the Comforter (Counselor, Helper, Intercessor, Advocate, Strengthener, Standby), the Holy Spirit, Whom the Father will send in My name [in My place, to represent Me and act on My behalf], He will teach you all things. And He will cause you to recall (will remind you of, bring to your remembrance) everything I have told you" (John 14:26, AMP).

What can we learn from the way Jesus advocates for us?

Jesus knew that His followers would feel lost without Him when He went to be with the Father, so He sent the Holy Spirit to fill that gap. The Spirit is a living conduit to God the Father. We, too, can stand in the gap between our children and where their hopes lie.

Sometimes the Spirit translates for us our innermost thoughts and feelings, those things we can't put into words. "In the same way the Spirit also helps our weakness; for we do not know how to pray as we should, but the Spirit Himself intercedes for us with groanings too deep for words" (Romans 8:26).

When my niece was three and four years old, we all had

trouble understanding her words. So many of them just didn't sound like any we used. I'd catch one word here and there; after a while I'd be able to figure out part of what she was trying to convey. She became more and more frustrated with our obvious inability to decipher her code.

The only one who didn't struggle to make sense of her mutterings was her older brother. When Kate ran through a string of syllables, we'd look at Nick. He would immediately translate, "She wants you to come outside with her and go on the swings." When Kate cried in frustration, Nick would say, "She just wants you to play a game with her." He even knew what she wanted to say when she was too upset to speak.

The Holy Spirit is like that for us. He knows us so well that when words fail to express our need in prayer, He offers His own on our behalf. He communicates to the Father with the intensity and clarity we feel but can't utter. He steps in when needed, but only in ways that advance God's plans for us.

"And He who searches the hearts knows what the mind of the Spirit is, because He intercedes for the saints according to the will of God" (Romans 8:27). The Spirit isn't going to champion something that God doesn't want to happen. He'd be working against our good and His purposes. So He reinforces God's promises and character when He pleads on our behalf.

In a similar way, I wouldn't be a good advocate for my child if I tried to advance something that was against my child's good and God's purposes. It may seem like a nice idea to get your child what he wants at this moment, but in the long run it may be detrimental to his character. Our instant society wants what it wants right now, but long-term values of persistence, perseverance, and patience are highly valued by God and a part of His design for us.

3. God the Father stands against those who stand against us. God is the greatest hero of all time. He can see into hearts and minds and defeat all enemies with a single word. He clears the path, points out the way, and goes with us on the journey. He stands between us and danger; we're safe with Him. "The LORD is my rock and my fortress and my deliverer, my God, my rock, in whom I take refuge; my shield and the horn of my salvation, my stronghold" (Psalm 18:2).

God isn't ignorant of our daily battles in this world. He's not a silent partner, but takes an active role in defending His children for our sakes and His glory.

We don't have to be perfect for Him to protect or defend us. There have been times when my children weren't blameless, yet I chose to stand up for them—or between them and someone who wished them harm. In fact, their own foolishness might have been part of the reason they needed protecting.

> How I choose to protect my children is just as important as whether I protect them or not.

When we play the role of protector, we often put ourselves and our reputations at risk. When our oldest was in seventh grade, he'd been picked on in the hallways by a bully who poked him incessantly as they passed between classes. One day Christopher, unable to take it anymore, swung around to confront his oppressor. In doing so, he inadvertently hit the boy in the face with his backpack.

Before Christopher could utter an apology, a teacher escorted both boys to the office. Following a "zero tolerance" policy on violence, the school punished my son along with his tormentor.

I went in to plead my son's case to the assistant principal. Our conversation didn't change the outcome, but it promoted a positive reputation for our family. The assistant principal wasn't used to seeing a protecting parent who wasn't out for blood!

I want my children to know, without a doubt, that they can trust me in times of trouble to be a protective shield. But that trust is twofold—trust in my ability to protect them, and trust in my character. *How* I choose to protect them is just as important as whether I protect them or not.

Since God is perfect, modeling our protective actions after His helps assure that we won't protect in the wrong way. It's all too easy when we sense that our children are threatened to get angry and act only out of that anger.

Our children don't always want us to come to their rescue, of course. We need to remember that sometimes God refrains from taking action because in the long run it's better that we learn to stand on our own.

Since our children are older now, it's important that I know first that my intervention is welcomed. It may be more important to your child that he handle an attack on his character himself than to have you run in like the cavalry. You might even make things worse.

One of the most loving pictures of God I have is running to safety under the shelter of His wings. Do your children feel that home is their safe place? Do they know they can always come to you, even when they're in trouble? There's no way your kids will trust you to be on their side if you haven't created a safe haven first.

God's love, strength, presence, and ability to get the job done encourage me to rely on Him. He's faithful and just in His dealings with me and even with my enemies. I can trust His protection.

That's how our children should feel about our protection, too.

The Imperfect Advocate

God is the perfect champion.

We aren't.

In our efforts to imitate God's model of flawless advocacy, we often fail. Sometimes it's because we're more interested in revenge than in our child's welfare. Sometimes it's because we doubt our abilities as parents; we cry "Uncle!" when the teacher questions our judgment, or shrink before the way-too-competitive coach who says our son doesn't have what it takes to win.

You're not a perfect advocate, but as a parent you know your child better than any other human does. You love him more than any other human could. And you have a higher stake in his future than any other human ever will.

It's true that we depend on others to help us navigate this parenting maze, but the "experts" are guides, not gods. Even though I'm a teacher who believes she knows more about her profession than a parent does, I also know that a parent knows more about his or her child than I do. Your child has been entrusted to you to love and raise. It's your calling, your vocation—and God always equips those He calls.

If you believe in God's sovereignty, you must believe you're not a parent by accident—even if you didn't plan it. The most careful planning doesn't ensure a sense of certainty about what feels sometimes like a grand experiment. You try one approach to see what happens, then adjust the variables and hope for a better outcome. You make mistakes.

Even if you feel unsteady on your feet as a parent, you'll grow stronger and steadier as you follow God's example of advocacy. Someone born with the grace of a dancer still needs to learn the steps to a dance. Talent may arrive at birth, but becoming a good dancer comes with practice.

Whether your children are 18 days or 18 years old, you can grow into a stable and balanced advocate. Trust your Creator and the truth of your own creation, and live up to His call on your life.

> As a parent you know your child better than any other human does.

If you're a Christian parent, you have a leader to follow. There's a lot at stake. When you stand up for your child, are you a sweet aroma to those you encounter—or an odor that repels the very people you need on your side?

When you approach the administrative assistant in the front office at your child's school or leave the bleachers to beckon the coach to speak with you at the fence, what goes through their minds? Do they smile at the prospect of meeting with you, or do they look for a place to hide? What reputation have you gained as a parent? This reputation influences the outcome of your advocacy more than you may realize—not to mention the image people have of the One to whom you belong.

No, we're not perfect. But our model is. You'll find echoes of His approach in many of the guiding principles that follow.

3

THE BUDDY,
THE BULLY, AND
THE HERO

Guiding Principle #1:
Be mindful of what you model.

"I'll go to the school from now on," my husband, Chip, said.

"But you don't understand the situation like I do," I protested.

"Exactly. That way I can walk in like every other ignorant parent and demand some answers!"

There was no changing his mind. He was going in to talk to those teachers himself. I was just afraid he'd burst in like a bull in a china closet—a closet I'd so carefully arranged.

Our youngest child, Charles, had been falling behind in his work. After multiple attempts to enlist his teachers' help with no success, we knew it was time to make a stronger stand on his behalf. I knew the teachers were already a little tired of hearing from me, though I'd approached them with respect each time.

But Charles was drowning, and we couldn't sit back and watch it happen.

"Just try to be nice," I suggested to Chip.

"Being 'nice' has gotten us where we are," he said. "Nowhere. It's time for a more direct approach."

"But remember that Miss Kendra is new this year, and Mr. Ross has been out sick a lot," I said.

"That's the problem," Chip said. "You know too much. You're too understanding."

It was true. As a teacher, I knew the frustrations and failings these people faced every day. I knew what would ruffle their feathers and what would smooth them over. Unfortunately, all that knowledge didn't seem to do my son much good. He was still misunderstood and misplaced.

> I wasn't convinced that my husband's "direct" approach would make things better.

Still, I wasn't convinced that my husband's "direct" approach would make things better. All I could picture was feathers flying everywhere!

I literally sat on my hands while my husband went to school. I was tempted to call him and tell him what to say. But knowing that at this point he wouldn't listen, I sat until my fingers grew numb.

Finally the phone rang.

"I walked right into the office and said I wanted to see certain teachers," Chip reported. "I told them I wasn't going anywhere until I saw them."

I cringed. This wasn't how I would have handled it.

"Did you see them?" I asked.

"I saw two of them and I told them my concerns," he said.

"Did you interrupt their classes, or did you wait to see them alone?"

"What does that matter? I made myself clear. That's all that matters."

But it did matter. I tried to put myself in the place of those teachers. How would I respond if a parent showed up at my class, uninvited and unannounced, expecting answers I didn't have?

The hairs on the back of my neck stood up. I knew this couldn't end well. But my way hadn't worked either. What should we do now?

Your Stand-up Style

When it comes to being an advocate, all parents are not the same. We don't take the same approach to problems. We don't interact with those in authority the same way. These differences can be good—if they're handled with care.

For example, I tend to let others' actions shape the way I interact with them. In an attempt to gain their approval I try to speak their language, follow their rules, and behave as they expect me to.

On the other hand, my husband, Chip, isn't looking for anyone's approval. He often suspects others are manipulating information or their image in order to lead him to a false conclusion.

When Chip and I find ourselves needing to stand up for our children, our competing views can get in the way of a united front. He might be seen as a "bully"; I might be seen as a "buddy." But as you'll see, neither approach makes for the most effective advocate.

These differences in style can help or hinder your cause. If you strive to find a balanced style to model for your children, you'll have a greater chance at success when you stand together for their sakes.

Three Kinds of Parents

I'm sure you've heard comments like, "She's certainly her mother's daughter," or, "He's definitely his father's son." When I conducted parent-teacher conferences, it was always a revealing experience; I could finally see where these kids got their habits from.

For better and for worse, most kids grow up to be very much like their parents. That can be an ego-building or ego-shattering thought!

It's also a good reason to consider what kind of advocate you are.

When you stand up for your child's needs, what role do you play? Do you sidle up to a teacher or coach and try to schmooze your way into his or her good graces to get your child what he needs? Or do you walk in ready for a fight—and get one?

Effective advocacy may depend on which persona you put forth. Being friendly or fearsome will get you only so far. Besides, you'll need to adjust to the different personalities you'll encounter.

Certain people respond best to certain personalities. It's not always possible, of course, to bring that ideal personality to the table. For example, if your son's soccer coach has a strong-willed, aggressive personality—and you don't—backing off from a much-needed confrontation will be seen as cowardice, not diplomacy. It might be time to send in the cavalry, enlisting the help of a partner who's more comfortable dealing with the coach.

But what if you're "it"? What if it's up to you to stand, like David in the Bible, against Goliath?

Whether you have the backup of a spouse or not, you can learn from the strategies employed in three common styles of advocacy. Each has strengths you can borrow and weaknesses you can avoid.

Style #1: The Buddy

The Buddy befriends before negotiation and puts that friendship ahead of his or her own needs. The Buddy's aim is to please, making accommodations in her speech, actions, and sometimes values in order to reach her goal.

The Buddy's mission is to understand the other person's point of view and use that information to reach her own objectives. The Buddy nurtures relationship above all else. She believes the best about people and their intentions, values approval, and sacrifices her desires for the sake of others. She places a high value on grace, offering second chances and multiple benefits of the doubt.

The Buddy has traits that Jesus Himself exemplifies, but no one is that easy to categorize. Even the Buddy is three-dimensional; there's another side to her temperament and tendencies.

Sometimes the Buddy can be perceived as weak and easy to manipulate. Her relatively mild personality may not instill confidence during negotiation—and can work to erode her position as advocate.

The Buddy also may be surprised by others' selfish and sometimes destructive agendas—so much so that she becomes paralyzed. Her focus on pleasing others may lead her away from her goal of advocacy. Sometimes the Buddy gives in to peer pressure for the sake of inclusion, even as an adult. And overemphasizing grace can permit others to get away with wrongdoing, possibly hurting the ones she is charged to defend and protect.

Do you recognize Buddy tendencies in yourself? I certainly do in myself. Even though we're all imprinted with a desire to please, that desire has driven too many of my thoughts and actions. Wanting to be included, not left out, I sometimes made choices for my children that reflected that desire.

Deciding to confront a teacher who wasn't meeting one of my sons' needs became a real issue for me. Having been a teacher in the very district my children attended, I knew what the teachers' lives were like. I knew their daily struggles, their frustrations, what they couldn't control.

I made excuses for them when they graded my son unfairly, penalized him for being absent, or didn't teach what needed to be taught. If they didn't return my phone calls or e-mails, I reminded myself how hard it was to stay on top of every communication. They were overwhelmed with paperwork, new to the school, faced too many discipline problems, had no support from parents or the administration.

Even now I could add to the list of excuses. But the bottom line was that I wanted to be included in their ranks, to still be considered a teacher when I no longer had a classroom of my own. I wanted so much to please them that my children's needs took a backseat.

So where is the balance for the Buddy?

The Buddy needs to develop more leadership qualities to offset her default position of follower. Two of these qualities are

(1) having a clear vision or mission, and (2) asserting personal values.

The Buddy knows how to listen and work cooperatively, but isn't as effective in defining her goals and making decisions based on her personal values. She may know her goal at the pediatrician's office is to make sure her son is tested for diabetes, for instance, but doesn't clearly communicate that to the doctor.

She may value traits like honesty, kindness, and faithfulness, but finds herself going along with the crowd at a PTA meeting when one of her son's teachers is wrongly accused. The Buddy has trouble voicing her values and opinions because she fears losing the friendship of the experts in her child's life. She also doesn't want to make waves or "cause trouble" because she believes it might jeopardize her child's experiences with the doctor, coach, teacher, grandparent, or friend.

The better choice is to explain clearly to all those involved where you stand, what you believe, and what your hopes are for the outcome of this interchange. No principal, judge, or church youth worker can read your mind, and won't know where you're coming from unless you tell him or her.

In many advocacy situations, silence means agreement. If you don't agree with how the "other side" is choosing to meet or ignore your child's needs, you must be willing to open your mouth and say so.

The Buddy has many positive attributes. If anyone would do well to adopt some of them, it's our next stand-up style.

Style #2: The Bully

Let's be clear: I'm not suggesting that becoming a Bully is in anyone's best interest. Nor am I saying that anyone with assertive tendencies is a Bully. For purposes of this discussion, the Bully is a set of personality traits—not a person.

Sometimes all of us want our own way, regardless of how it affects anyone else. The Bully tends to do this a lot more often than the Buddy. The Bully believes strongly in his own opinion, and operates with a high level of certainty about what he does and why. He makes decisions quickly and takes action the same way.

The Bully makes decisions quickly and takes action the same way.

He lives in a black-and-white world and believes everyone else should, too. He thinks life is not that complicated and solutions should be simple. Others may see him as someone who knows his own mind and is in charge. Confidence defines his demeanor and actions; when it's used wisely, he's often seen as a leader.

The word *bully* conjures up an oversized, overindulged boy or girl who picks on smaller, weaker kids. Yet the Bully has positive traits that can help him get what his children need.

The Bully is persuasive, stating his case concisely and without hesitancy. He's seldom influenced by what others think of him or affected by peer pressure. He stands tall, assured that his way is best. Strong-willed and at times defiant, the Bully pushes ahead through the waters of adversity.

The Bully will not be swayed from his mission. To accomplish it, he bulldozes the rest of us with the fact that he is bigger, better, louder, quicker, or smarter than we are.

The Bully always has to have the last word, too.

It's no mistake that I said my husband rushed in like a bull in a china closet. He has many Bully traits, but never could be considered an actual bully. The problem comes when the Bully is not aware of the effect he has on others.

The Bully doesn't always get his way, though. Society will tolerate only so much from him.

Chip and I saw an example of this recently in an expensive restaurant. Waiting to be seated, we couldn't help but overhear an elderly female customer ranting to the hostess. I watched in horror as this woman pummeled the 18-year-old hostess with overblown complaints about her meal. She was not only rude; she was abusive in her speech and invasive in her physical proximity.

When the manager arrived, the complainer didn't take a breath before turning her attack on him. Finally, even though the woman was well into her 70s, the manager said he would physically remove her from the premises if she didn't leave of her own accord.

Soon he was on the phone with the police as two of his wait staff led the woman out of the building by her elbows. She continued to spew toxic words that fell on the ears of many other patrons. Her browbeaten husband followed her out of the restaurant—at least ten paces behind. It was obvious that he'd learned long ago to keep his mouth shut and stay out of her way.

Why do some people push the limits of civilized behavior in order to get what they want or think they need? Perhaps it's because their pushy natures usually got them what they wanted when they were children, so they rely on it well into adulthood.

The Bully parent—whether showing up in the doctor's waiting room, at soccer practice, or in the front office at school—is considered a "nightmare parent." Those of us who serve the needs of children try to avoid the Bully at all costs; sometimes the cost is not meeting the needs of the child. So even though the Bully thinks he's getting his way, doctors, coaches, teachers, and even friends look for ways *not* to interact with him at all.

How can the Bully get balanced?

The Bully must temper his aggressiveness with some selfless traits if he's to advocate effectively for his children. He could benefit from adopting cooperative qualities like (1) a willingness to serve others, (2) learning to listen, and (3) negotiating toward agreement. It's a matter of becoming "other-minded," stepping outside oneself and seeing the needs of others.

The Bully needs to learn how to really participate in others' lives, not just direct them. For example, it's seldom productive to march into the school office and demand answers from a teacher you've never met. First spend time serving on a committee or helping in the classroom, seeing the inner workings before you pass judgment. Serve not just to gather information about your "adversaries," but to gain insight and understanding.

Would those who know you say that you have an overpowering personality that tends to monopolize the conversation? If so, develop listening skills. Effective communication relies on both speaking and listening; they're two sides of the same coin. Sometimes the Bully is so focused on what he wants or needs to say that he doesn't even hear the other person.

If you have Bully tendencies, remind yourself to really listen when someone else is speaking. Ask questions instead of making statements. Ask in order to clarify your understanding and to seek new information.

Paying attention to your nonverbal behavior also can help you become a better listener. Make eye contact with the speaker.

Keep your hands still and your body facing the person, so he knows he has your attention. This helps you really listen instead of pretending to listen while you formulate your next statement.

Avoid monologues, too. Have you ever noticed a character in a book, on television, on stage, or on film who talks for the sake of talking? People like this love their words, and believe persuasion results from allowing a long, continuous strand of them to flow unfiltered from their mouths.

Nothing could be further from the truth. Just as we tire of fictional characters who monologize, our doctors, coaches, teachers, and spouses tune out in the presence of those who do it in real life.

Bullies also have the tendency to overwhelm others with their point of view. But negotiation is a necessary skill for effective advocacy. The Bully has mastered the first part of negotiation—*assertiveness*. He just has to use it to speak up for truth instead of pushing his opinion in a way that may harm others.

Another element of negotiation is *consideration*—seeing others' feelings as being just as important as your own. This doesn't mean that you put aside your feelings in favor of others', but that you consider others' feelings seriously before choosing your next move. This is not easy for the Bully, but will enable him to be the negotiator his children need him to be.

Finally, it's important to be *flexible* in negotiations. This means being open to new ideas and opinions, willing to change your mind. This shakes the Bully to the very core; he believes his way is the right way! But learning to bend in response to someone else's needs can be a win-win situation; as in a dance, the Bully can lead in a way that makes both partners look good.

The Bully has the strength to lead and persuade, if he's

careful. But the advocate we all look to and hope to be for our children is embodied in our third style.

Style #3: The Hero

The Buddy and the Bully may envision themselves as heroes, but both fall short.

The true Hero is self-sacrificing, putting the needs of others first. He's competent and trusted by others to get the job done. He's faithful to a fault, unable to stop himself from jumping in and saving victims.

The Hero does the tasks no one else will do, puts in more hours than anyone else is willing to spend, and goes above and beyond the call of duty. You can always count on him. He's defined by his humility, uncomfortable with praise. "I'm just doing my job," he often says.

When the situation is darkest, the Hero appears and turns on the lights. Motivated by the greater good, he believes that the needs of the many outweigh the needs of the one (his).

As admirable as these traits are, the Hero isn't perfect. He has some things to learn if he's to stand up effectively for his children.

The Hero is sometimes too busy saving the world to attend to his family's needs. It's not that he thinks family members' needs aren't important; it's that he believes those needs will take care of themselves. He believes his job is a unique calling and requires 110 percent of himself to get it done.

He may or may not be a workaholic, but his time is definitely spread too thin. He may be the president of the PTA, director of the Little League, or a cardiac surgeon who's been convinced that the world would stop turning without him.

He is usually an ordinary person who does extraordinary

things. Many people count on him, and he's there when they need him. No call for help goes unanswered; no request is too unreasonable.

The Hero's quest is noble, but makes it hard to sustain his primary relationships. Consider fictional heroes. An ordinary person feels unsatisfied; after losing someone or something he loves, he goes out in search of his destiny, the meaning for his existence. He learns what he must do to overcome bigger and bigger obstacles—until he finally has to sacrifice himself to triumph and realize his place in this world. He is a savior, a champion of the people.

Many firefighters, police officers, medical personnel, ministers, teachers, and politicians are driven by the hero's tale. Unfortunately, though the children of heroes admire their parents' abilities, they secretly wish they were the focus of their parents' efforts.

In many ways Jesus is the prime example of the hero's tale. Unlike others, however, He's perfect. For one thing, He was— and continues to be—able to sustain His relationships.

How can the Hero save the world without losing touch with his own child?

He needs to (1) spend a little time reflecting on how he does what he does and how it affects his family, and (2) look for ways to improve his closest relationships.

Without reflection and strong relationships, even a Hero can't be an effective advocate for his children. Better to question your own motives and behaviors before others do—and they will.

How often do we see the Hero—perhaps an athlete, president, or televangelist—whose own house is not in order? Even Princess Diana, much as I admired her as an incredible humanitarian, spent less and less time with her boys in order to save children around the world. Each of us who spends time and energy being the "answer to prayer" for our churches, schools, and other causes needs to take a closer look at our priorities.

When our stated priorities and our actions don't match, psychologists call it *dissonance*. If we claim to put our families first, yet work harder and longer to meet the needs of other families, that's dissonance. This creates tension in ourselves and those we love; to alleviate it, we either change our words to match our actions, or change our actions to match our words.

Seek to be a hero to your kids before trying to be a Hero to the outside world. God's glory is the only glory that matters, so ask Him to point out any dissonance in your life. If you've been seeking your own glory, even unwittingly, He'll reveal it to you.

The Hero flirts with pride and sometimes succumbs to it. That happened to me, and it threatened to extinguish any faith my children had in my ability to stand up for them.

As a teacher who had school-age children, I believed I knew best—not just for my children, but for all the children in their school. I volunteered there so often that the principal joked that he should pay me. I headed committees, held office in the PTA, volunteered in the classroom and the office, substitute-taught when I could, taught parent workshops, edited the school newsletter, and chaperoned field trips. The school was grateful for my help; I was great at filling gaps.

God revealed my pride when it became clear that my own son's needs were not being met. Unchallenged at school, he began to shut down academically and stopped caring. His teacher seemed uninterested in finding out how to meet his needs.

My deflation came when I finally stepped in to offer the

school insight into how my son learned and what would motivate him. His teachers were not impressed with my teaching expertise or how many volunteer hours I'd logged. I was trying to cross into their territory, and they stood guard like the border patrol of an unfriendly country.

My attempts to advocate for my son's needs failed. The principal who'd been so grateful for my help said, "I can't make my teachers do what they don't want to do. I guess we can't help you here."

Pride went before a fall. I certainly fell flat on my face that semester.

Even the Hero can benefit from some improvement. Are you willing to look honestly at your weaknesses and make changes to become the champion your child really needs? Your plan for improvement may begin with seeking forgiveness from God and from family members you've inadvertently injured.

The Buddy, the Bully, and the Hero all have the same goal—to step in and do what's necessary to get their children's needs met. If you have Buddy tendencies, let your kids see you developing more leadership qualities. If you have Bully tendencies, let them see you learning how to work more cooperatively. If you're known in your community as a Hero, let them see you making your family a top priority.

Standing Together

Buddies don't necessarily marry Buddies. Bullies may not be attracted to Bullies. Heroes don't always find each other.

So what should you do when your stand-up styles clash?

If you're married, you shouldn't be a lone-ranger advocate.

Two parents presenting a united front while standing up for their children are more effective than one standing alone. As the saying goes, "United, we stand; divided, we fall."

The same is true for parents who must advocate in an especially difficult or emotional situation—when facing a child's expulsion from school or a life-threatening illness, for example. One spouse may handle stress more easily or may know more about the problem. Dividing your advocacy responsibilities is fine, but dividing your partnership isn't. Keep your spouse in the loop.

In some families, anything related to the kids is considered "mom's territory"; dad takes a hands-off approach. In other families, mom handles all things connected to school and friends; dad takes care of sports concerns. In still other families, spouses try to take on doctor visits and parent-teacher conferences as equally as their schedules allow.

However you divvy up the responsibilities, what matters is that you communicate regularly about what's going on in your realm. If your partner must negotiate in your place, make sure he or she doesn't enter the fray without the facts.

Despite differences in style, it's important that parents are more or less of the same mind when negotiating. Most caregivers and service providers prefer to take the path of least resistance; if one of you tends to back down, they'll try to take advantage of that by interacting mainly with the acquiescent parent.

Here are some guidelines on presenting a confident, united front when standing up for your child.

1. *Arrive and leave together.* Sometimes this can't be done, but strive to show up at meetings on time—and at the same

time. Tensions rise when people are late, and arriving at different times may be taken as an indication that one parent hasn't
made this meeting a priority. Try to
leave together, too, instead of having
one partner slip out early—and giving the impression that you're not
very serious about the matter at
hand.

If you've been the primary advocate so far, bring your partner up to speed.

   2. *Come to the table prepared.* Make
sure you both understand the purpose of the appointment. If you've been the primary advocate so far, bring your
partner up to speed. If you need documents, bring them. A
sense of unity shatters when one partner is furiously searching
for papers he or she was supposed to bring.

   3. *Never argue with or undermine your partner in front of caregivers or service providers.* Any disagreement you have with your
partner about the issue at hand should be handled in private.
Reach consensus before setting foot in the room. Avoid saying
things like, "My husband doesn't understand the pressure you're
under," or, "My wife doesn't grasp medical terminology very
easily." Your job is to build your partner up and protect his or
her reputation. This helps to solidify your position as parents.

   4. *Share "talk time."* Does one of you tend to monopolize
conversations? Unity is in question if only one partner speaks
while the other sits quietly like a submissive child. If you dread
talking because you fear a confrontation, prepare a few questions ahead of time to guide you. Even if you know more about
the situation, it's important to give your partner equal time.

   5. *Have a secret signal for "bad" behavior.* Some of us overuse
sarcasm, go down rabbit trails, or revert to name-calling during

uncomfortable conversations. If the "bad" behavior continues, it jeopardizes your credibility and your position. My husband and I give each other secret signals when we've wandered down the wrong path during a conversation. I gently put my hand on his knee; he makes eye contact with me and smiles. When this happens, he knows he needs to reel himself in—and I know I need to get back to the point.

Don't Get Typecast

Depending on our style, we tend to either charge like bulls or tiptoe like sly children into advocacy. We say, "It's my nature," or "That's how I've always handled things."

Rules of Negotiation

1. Know what you're willing to do and not do.
2. Do as well as you can for your child.
3. Get as much information as you can.
4. Stay calm, cool, and collected.
5. Don't be competitive just to be competitive.
6. Know when to cooperate.
7. Work with the power you have.
8. Decide ahead of time what the most important outcome is.
9. Think at least one step ahead.
10. When it's over, it's over.[1]

We don't have to be prisoners of our tendencies. For the sake of our kids, we mustn't be. How we stand up for them speaks volumes to caregivers and service providers—and to the children who look to us as models they'll emulate someday.

4

ONCE UPON A TIME

Guiding Principle #2:
*Know intimately the needs of both sides
before you speak for either.*

Susan watched and waited to see whether things would be different this time. Jeremy, her 12-year-old, still sat on the bench at the soccer field. It was the second half, and Coach Harding had promised that each child would play in this game.

The coach paced back and forth, running his frenzied fingers through his thinning hair. Susan could see him check his watch every few minutes.

At least he's paying attention to how much time these kids have been on the field.

Five minutes. Ten minutes. Twenty minutes passed, and still the coach didn't call a time out. Susan squirmed in her seat. There were only two games left in the season. She could tell that Jeremy had given up hope; he was playing "Rock, Paper, Scissors" with a fellow benchwarmer.

With only five minutes left in the game, Susan couldn't take it anymore. She'd promised herself she'd sit still and keep her mouth shut this time, but that was after the coach had assured her that Jeremy would play today.

What was the matter with Coach Harding, anyway? He'd canceled more practices than he'd held, and forfeited two games. Whenever he did show up, he was preoccupied or on his cell phone. Now he'd broken his promise again. Susan decided all bets were off.

She didn't deserve this treatment, after all. At this point in the season many parents had stopped showing up for games; out of sixteen players, only the parents of four attended regularly. The lack of support irked Susan, who showed up for every practice, every game, every award ceremony. She always made sure the team had fresh orange quarters and water at halftime, and even collected money to give Coach Harding a plaque for this season. Why did she invest so much time and energy in supporting a coach who seemed to care so little about her kid?

She packed up her cooler and collapsible camping chair and stowed them in her car. By the time she returned, the game was over. Ready to confront Coach Harding for what she hoped would be the last time, she instructed Jeremy to wait for her in the car.

But Coach Harding had vanished! She turned in time to see his funky lime green Volkswagen turn out of the recreation center's parking lot.

Her best friend, Natalie, walked up behind her. "Well, that's probably the last we'll see of him."

"I'll catch him during Tuesday's practice," Susan muttered. She had every word scripted for the occasion.

"No, you won't. He's not coming back. It's over."

"He can't just quit! He can't just leave these kids high and dry. Jeremy still hasn't played!"

"Susan, give the man a break," Natalie said. "His wife just died!"

Susan froze.

"I . . . didn't know," she finally whispered, as if afraid to break a sacred silence.

No wonder Coach wasn't focused on the game or the needs of any of his players, let alone her son. No wonder he'd canceled so many practices.

No wonder.

"There are always two sides to a story," a mother cautions.

"You'd think differently about him if you heard her story," a best friend insists.

"No one ever wants to hear the bad guy's story," a prison inmate gripes to his cellmate.

"Now that you've listened to the prosecutor's story, give me the courtesy of your attention for ours," the defense attorney opens.

The desire to be heard is strong. Yet many of us, like Coach Harding, walk away with our stories untold.

Standing up for our children requires storytelling. The better we are at telling our stories and listening to those of others, the better our chances that all parties will get what they need.

Some failed attempts at advocacy are a result of poor storytelling. If we leave out important details, there's a good chance the "other side" won't get the point. If we alter details to ingratiate or even distance ourselves, we'll win or lose under false pretenses.

Some of us don't tell our stories at all for fear of appearing weak or to keep our opponents "in the dark." Sometimes, wrapped up in our own stories, we don't even consider that others have important stories to tell. But telling and hearing stories gives us information that helps us negotiate and make decisions about our children.

Everyone has a story to tell. Yours is important, as are the stories of those you interact with—especially those who interact with your kids.

The Power of Story

If you doubt how powerful stories can be, consider courtrooms—where stories are showcased for better and for worse. Even potential jurors must tell their stories before being chosen to listen to the stories of the defense and prosecution. The judge has his own story; if it collides with the case at hand, he might be asked to excuse himself from the proceedings. Stories influence the outcome of many cases—in court and in standing up for your child.

Jesus told stories. His parables were meant to either illuminate or cloud the minds of his audiences. He didn't reveal His own story right away, even to those closest to Him. He was strategic in His storytelling. We can be, too.

How important is it to know someone else's story when standing up for your child? How crucial is it that the person on the other side of the table, desk, or sideline knows yours?

If you don't know the other person's story, you'll tend to make one up for her anyway. You'll make assumptions about motives and intentions, judging unspoken attitudes and values as less admirable than your own. If the other person doesn't know your story, she'll do the same for you.

That's why it's so vital that we know each other's stories. Then we can negotiate based on truth—not fiction.

When It's Tough to Tell Your Story

When she heard of the death of Coach Harding's wife, Susan finally admitted, "I didn't know." She wasn't aware of his story because he'd chosen not to share it.

Where does sharing your story fall on the continuum between complete privacy and full disclosure? Many of us have been taught not to "air dirty laundry" or "wear your heart on your sleeve"; sharing the personal stories of our lives doesn't come easily to us.

Common ground is tilled by shared experiences.

In my own family, stories had to be pulled out of their owners bit by bit, almost like digging for a splinter. It was painful, but in the end everyone felt better.

My grandmother, for example, had a hard life growing up in New York as the daughter of Italian immigrants. It was full of difficult circumstances and even tragedy. "Better to forget," she'd tell me when I'd ask about her past. "Today is what's important."

But I really wanted to know her story—the reasons why she responded to family issues as she did, why she treated those closest to her as she did. She was a mystery to me, and her reactions often caught me off guard.

I knew family was important to her, but it seemed she held us all in a death grip. Her love was suffocating; for some of us, the only way to breathe again was to escape. Those who grew up with her knew her stories. They understood her in a way I never could—and were never surprised by how she handled anything.

Had I known my grandmother's story, I would have been better able to understand her motives and values. When I lived with her, I saw her as an obstacle to overcome—an adversary. My ability to stand up for myself in her presence was severely handicapped because I didn't know her story and she didn't know mine. It wasn't until years later that I caught a glimpse of her story and began to understand her.

Not wanting to appear vulnerable is one reason we find it hard to share our stories. This is especially true for those in positions of power or influence—whether parents, professors, politicians, police officers, or pediatricians. Stories might reveal chinks in our armor, making us appear less capable.

As a teacher I tried to keep my personal story separate from my professional one. I didn't want one life to bleed into the other; I was afraid it would put my credibility into question. I've discovered since that your personal story helps you appear more human, more approachable, even more credible. Common ground is tilled by shared experiences, and common ground is needed in any negotiation.

Sharing your story when you stand up for your child can build mutual understanding and respect. If you want to be an effective advocate, those ingredients are a must. Without mutual understanding there's discomfort, tension, strife. Wars begin when we don't know both sides of the story.

Overcoming Storytelling Fears

If you're reluctant to tell your story, what would it take to change your mind?

Maybe you want assurance that others won't use your story

to hurt you. You're afraid that, as arresting officers declare, "Anything you say can and will be used against you in a court of law."

The truth is that you won't get that assurance. You can hope others will treat your story with respect—and trust God with the rest. All parties have to accept the fact that they do this with no guarantees of safety.

To begin the process, you may need to take off your mask. I mean the one you wear like a superhero protecting her secret identity. You need to let others see you as the everyday person you are—familiar, human, fairly approachable.

If I don't take off my mask, you won't believe my story even if I tell you. With the mask off, you'll see that I'm a mom who worries about her kids and wants the best for them, who'll go to great lengths to protect them, and who's willing to be transparent if that's what it takes to get their needs met. You'll see that I'm a woman of faith who struggles every day to see God in the details of her life and those of her children. I'm a wife who battles a poor self-image and wonders why her husband loves her. With the mask off, you see my imperfections and insecurities like the freckles on the porcelain complexion of a redhead.

What it really takes for you and me to share our stories is to be willing to take a risk. Coach Harding believed it wasn't appropriate to share that he was a husband trying to keep it together while his wife was dying at home. When I consider whether or not to open the book of my life to a caregiver or service provider, I need to ask myself, "What's the worst thing that could happen if I tell my story?"

Once I generate a few answers to that question, I need to ask myself, "Can I live with that?" More than likely I can, with God's help—and so can you.

Stories We Tell Ourselves

What tends to happen when we face a problem with someone in our children's lives? First, we recognize that this person doesn't agree with us. Then we tell ourselves an "ugly" story about that person. Then we throw an accusation his way.[1]

Why do we tell ourselves an "ugly" story? It's the easiest way to explain the fact that the person doesn't agree with us. Often when dealing with the needs of our children, we get overprotective; the mother-bear phenomenon overcomes us, and we charge in with fangs flashing.

More than likely the "ugly" story is nowhere close to the real one. And once we shoot an accusation at our opponents, there's a good chance they'll tell themselves an "ugly" story about us. Both sides end up feeling disrespected.

Consider this story from a father I'll call Matt.

When my son was in the third grade, they had an open house. They made aliens out of paper plates, construction paper, etc. The goal was for the parents to identify the alien their child had constructed. Jon was so happy that I could come, and I actually picked out his alien. His mood was great and it was fun. Then I asked him to show me his desk. He turned white as a ghost and became very quiet. He pointed to the corner away from the other students' desks.

I went to the teacher and asked why my son's desk was in the corner away from everyone else. She explained that he had problems working in a group.

I asked how isolating him would help him with his group interaction skills. She obviously became defensive.

I asked her to define the problem. The first response was that since he was out of the classroom often as part of the Talented and Gifted (TAG) group, he usually wasn't there for the entire time. She also said that when she passed out worksheets to complete, he would often finish them before she had finished handing them out to the other students. I asked her if they were correct. Her response was that it didn't matter because she wanted him to take longer since she didn't have anything else for him to do until the other students were finished. Her solution was to "reward" him with additional work not required of the other students.

My son did not see this as a reward but as a punishment, and there were some resulting behavioral problems. We tried to resolve the situation with the teacher directly. Little things like handing the worksheets to Jon last or allowing self-selected reading during this time. [Or] moving his desk back!

The teacher refused. We went to the principal, who informed us that it was not her "style" to tell her teachers how to teach. My wife, a school teacher, told this story to her principal. Within an hour, my son was transferred to another school and enjoyed it. Unfortunately, to this day my son has been scarred by this. He lost his desire to be different by being smart, but prefers to just blend in.

What happened here?

Sometimes we don't tell the whole story, if we tell it at all. We may withhold crucial information because we feel the other party has violated our expectations. Once this happens, information is protected so that further violation won't occur.

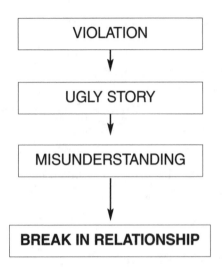

In Matt's case, the teacher basically shut down once he questioned her decision to move his son's desk away from the other students. Matt's question was a reaction to his feeling that the teacher had violated his expectations.

Because the teacher shut down, Matt made up her story on his own. He probably drew the wrong conclusions.

Matt admitted that even though he believed he spoke to the teacher in a respectful tone, more often than not he found himself interrupting her. He told himself that this teacher had it in for his son and was prejudiced against children in the gifted program—which meant she wouldn't be willing to meet his unique needs. He also told himself that he had the right to question the teacher's authority, and his anger was justified because he was protecting his son.

When it comes to others' stories, a simple guideline helps. Instead of making up someone else's story, try to get him to tell it to you himself.

How we talk to ourselves when we feel violated goes a long way in determining what we do next. This is true not only of the fables we make up about others, but the ones we invent about ourselves. Some of these stories help us feel better about ourselves; others make us feel worse. In Matt's case, he told himself many things to explain both his own and the teacher's behavior.

Then there are the stories we make up about our children. Sometimes we think the worst about our kids and overreact, but other times we think only the best and delude ourselves. The truth is usually somewhere in the middle.

Matt told himself that his son was beyond reproach in this situation. He acted with that belief in mind when talking to the teacher. We don't know whether Matt's assessment was true, but it *is* what he believed.

Getting the Story Straight

How can you make sure you're getting—and giving—stories accurately in the process of standing up for your child? Here are seven ways to stay on the straight and narrow.

1. *Don't invent stories to excuse or condemn opponents.* When the stakes are high, as they usually are when we advocate for our children, we may try to explain our opponents' behavior by telling ourselves stories that paint them in either a positive or negative light. If you long to reach mutual understanding, you may try to explain bad behavior with a fable. If you prefer to "keep your distance," you may be more callous in your judgment.

For example, when teachers reneged on a promise to help our son find ways to complete assignments with a broken wrist, I told myself they were overworked and overtired. Why? I wanted to ingratiate myself to them; I wanted us to all be friends. I told myself that this would make my son's life at school easier, that his teachers would be more willing to give him what he needed. I was wrong.

When we're caught up in conspiracy theories, our attempts at advocacy suffer.

When you have no desire to become friends with the opposing party, the temptation is to tell yourself a story that puts that party in the worst possible light. Neither approach is likely to lead to a meeting of the minds.

2. *Avoid conspiracy theories.* When others don't behave in a way that we approve, agree with, or expect, we look for a reason. Often we jump to conclusions. Sometimes we convince ourselves that our opponents are acting intentionally to harm us or our children.

When we're caught up in conspiracy theories, our attempts at advocacy suffer. Such theories distract us from the matter at hand—getting our children's needs met in a way that brings glory to God. We might consider His statement in Isaiah 8:12: "You are not to say, 'It is a conspiracy!' in regard to all that this people call a conspiracy, and you are not to fear what they fear or be in dread of it."

3. *Don't use stories to rationalize your own bad behavior.* There are times when we parents behave badly. Some of us turn into domestic kitties and hiss a bit; others morph into roaring lions or lionesses and go directly for the throat. How we spin this conduct doesn't turn it into a virtue.

Maybe you'd never pummel a baseball umpire to the ground

over a bad call, or point a gun at the assistant principal and demand that your son be released from detention. But if you're at all like me, you've dabbled in at least one of the following:

- talking behind your opponent's back
- spreading a rumor, or holding your tongue when a false accusation is uttered
- playing good cop/bad cop with your spouse in a meeting about your child
- conveniently missing an appointment the opposing party set up
- not answering a phone call, e-mail, or letter
- calling the opposing party at home late at night, or leaving multiple messages that escalate in intensity
- going over the other person's head instead of following the chain of command
- refusing eye contact, avoiding your opponent in the hallway, on the playing field, at the playground
- interrupting, using a condescending tone of voice, yelling, using abusive language, or name-calling
- circulating a petition against the person without trying to resolve the situation first
- showing up uninvited or unannounced for a confrontation, hoping to catch the person off guard
- using adversarial body language, "getting in their face," or making inappropriate or abusive physical contact
- anything that can be construed as harassment.

No, you didn't blow up your opponent's car. But isn't coveting another man's wife as bad as having an adulterous affair with her? Jesus says it is (Matthew 5:27-28). Isn't having malice in your heart toward another person as bad as killing that person? Again, Jesus says it is (Matthew 5:21-22).

I hate to tell you this, but there's really no good way to spin these stories to explain our bad behavior.

4. *Steer clear of false modesty.* I found this out the hard way when, during a meeting with one of our sons' teachers, I downplayed what I did for a living. Trying to endear myself, I mentioned that I was a teacher. I didn't mention that I was also a writer with 20 books, a plethora of articles, and a curriculum to my credit. That didn't serve me well when, later in the year, I needed to stand up for my son regarding his writing assignments in that teacher's class. Because I'd left writing expertise out of my story, I had no credibility with her in that area.

Your God-given gifts and experience are part of your story. Don't let your story be one of underestimated value.

5. *Don't exaggerate to make yourself look good.* All of us prefer to present a positive, and sometimes inflated, image of ourselves to the watching world. Even in the worst of situations, we want to come out "smelling like a rose," as my mother used to say.

That's why I'm thinking of coloring my hair. It's why, when I have to put together my "bio"—my story in a nutshell—I scour my memory for all the positive attributes and experience I can gather.

We tend to adjust our stories by cutting things out (pruning), by showcasing only the best parts (preening), or even exaggerating or embellishing (puffing up).

Consider the following conversation.

Sitting at the dining-room table with his wife and two friends, Andy declared, "I can't believe how thoughtless this teacher is. She had the gall to call us at home at midnight!"

"Ten o'clock," Andy's wife corrected in a whisper. "This is the fourth time this week she's called that late," he continued.

"Only the second time," his wife said under her breath.

"We're always in bed by 9:30 P.M., so this is a real intrusion," Andy said.

"Eleven P.M.," his wife corrected more loudly.

"Anyway, I gave her a piece of my mind this time, and told her in no uncertain terms that we wouldn't stand for this any longer. It borders on harassment!"

"You said no such thing," his wife countered. "If you'd returned the permission slip for the field trip tomorrow like you promised, she wouldn't have had to call us. And if you'd given her your work number, she wouldn't have to call us at home at all!"

When we inflate the facts to make ourselves look or sound better, we risk looking foolish. If an accusation or confrontation resulted from this conversation, Andy probably would "stick to his story"—until his distortions were revealed. When we tell our stories, we need to tell the whole truth.

But just so you know, I still intend to cover my gray!

6. *Don't let silence tell the story.* "Let them believe what they want," Angie told me. "It's none of their business anyway."

"But what's in this file makes assumptions about you that just aren't true," I insisted. "They think you don't care about your kids!"

As a parent liaison to the school system, I was trying to help Angie and her child's teachers come to a mutual understanding. But she wasn't giving me much to work with.

"They're going to think what they want, no matter what I say. So what's the point?" Angie asked.

"The point is that you're letting them write the story in this file. It's your story. You need to write it yourself."

The teachers didn't know Angie couldn't drive, that her husband worked the night shift, and that they had five children—three of them under the age of six. All they knew was that she hadn't shown up for the "mandatory" conferences they'd scheduled. Her oldest son struggled with a learning disability, but she couldn't attend all those meetings with social workers, school psychologists, special education teachers, guidance counselors, and district-level specialists. They concluded that she didn't want to participate in her son's education.

Henry David Thoreau said, "Nature abhors a vacuum." If you've created a hole in your story by keeping silent, someone else will fill it with her own assessment of who you are, what you believe, and what you want for your child.

7. *Strive to give a true reflection.* The truth may not always be as exciting as the stories other people make up about you, but at least it's the truth. Let the mirror really reflect you—warts and all.

The stories we tell about ourselves must be accurate if we're going to advocate effectively and with integrity for our children. When we misrepresent who we are to the watching world, we aren't fooling anyone. We just look foolish—to the ballet teacher, the pediatrician, and our kids.

How to Tell Your Story

"Okay," you say. "I need to tell my story, my child's story, and listen to the 'other side.' But how much of the story do I tell? And when?"

Exactly how and when you tell your story isn't as important as telling it. But here are two issues you should consider.

1. *Tell as much of the story as necessary to reach mutual understanding.*

If you tend to spew details, you'll probably want to exercise self-control when telling your story. More words don't always mean better. The more we say, the more susceptible we are to delusions of grandeur, going off on tangents, and letting our emotions instead of the truth guide our tongues.

Stories offer the "why" behind what you do.

If you're someone who usually keeps your mouth shut in confrontational situations, I encourage you to be brave enough to open it with wisdom. Prepare by role-playing in your mind, or even aloud.

Whether you relish the banter of debate or prefer the quiet of your own counsel, ask the Holy Spirit to choose your words and guide your speech. Tell your story judiciously, because every word counts when standing up for your child.

2. *Decide whether to tell your story as a prologue, a flashback, editorializing, or an epilogue.*

When it comes to timing, there are several approaches to telling your "backstory." Drawn from traditions followed by writers, they can have a powerful effect as we negotiate on behalf of our children.

Prologues appear at the beginning. In nonfiction, they're often the story behind the story—the reason for the book, and its premise. In fiction, a prologue often introduces key characters, begins to set up the plot, and otherwise intrigues the reader.

People who believe in the value of "getting things out in the open" tend to prefer the prologue approach when telling stories as part of standing up for their children.

There is a caution attached to the prologue approach, however. When you meet a coach, police officer, teacher, or college admissions decision maker for the first time, you may be tempted to tell your child's life story up front—thinking it will make all the difference. Try asking first whether or not it would benefit the listener if you told the story behind the story. If he gives you a green light, proceed freely. If he gives you a yellow light, proceed with caution and reveal *some* of the backstory. If he gives you a red light, stop immediately!

Flashbacks and *editorializing* are two ways to reveal backstory in the midst of a book. The former, usually found in fiction, steps out of the current scene to tell you about an important incident from the past. The latter, generally used in nonfiction, allows the author to comment directly to the reader.

Unfortunately, breaking the flow in this way can be distracting—in writing and in negotiating. An aggressive personality, wanting you to get to the point, may see your explanations as an annoying detour. A gentler personality may relish your periodic eye-openers and see them as opportunities to get to know you better.

If you sense that the "other side" is impatient with your flashbacks and editorializing, try leaving your backstory for the end.

Epilogues tell "the rest of the story." They appear at the end of a book. Sometimes they're the best place to relate your backstory; sometimes they're the only place.

For example, our youngest son missed a day of school in order to attend a school chorus function. He ended up with a lot of class work to make up, but couldn't complete it on time. He should have told his teacher about his struggle before the deadline arrived, but didn't. After he received poor grades on the missed work, I told him to explain to the teacher why he didn't meet her expectations. His epilogue did earn him a reprieve—that time, anyway.

Stories offer the "why" behind what you do. Explaining the "why" behind your requests doesn't guarantee success, no matter when you do the explaining. If nothing else, though, it may help to prevent future problems.

The more you know about those with whom you interact, the more you'll know about how and when to reveal your story to them.

They Can't Read Your Mind

So why should we tell and listen to stories as we stand up for our kids? Because we're not mind readers.

That person sitting at the other end of the table, standing on the other side of the Little League field's fence, or looking at you from across your kitchen counter can't read your mind—and you can't read hers. Without stories, we can only wonder, "Why would a sensible, rational person do such a thing?" With stories, we can discover what's going on with that person to explain why he's doing what he's doing. This offers a real opportunity to work together.

My husband and I recently accepted this truth. I was in the habit of staying quiet about my feelings, getting disappointed that Chip didn't read my mind and meet my needs. Chip, without a clue as to why I would back away at those times, would leave me to my solitude. No mutual understanding there.

Finally, to avoid further miscommunication, unmet expectations, and failed attempts at unity, we made a pact. We both promised not to expect mind reading. I promised to tell him what I felt when I was feeling it; he promised to ask me more questions so he could better understand my backstory.

Sounds like a plan for advocacy, too, doesn't it?

5

KNOWING WHEN TO STEP IN

Guiding Principle #3:
*Keep the long-term best interests of your child in mind
when you make short-term decisions to intercede.*

"He hates me!" Natalie finally blurted to her mom after the longest silence on record.

All Carol had wanted to know was why Natalie got a C in her advanced chemistry class.

"He doesn't hate you," Carol soothed. "He's just not very personable."

Carol remembered the first time she'd met Mr. Hayden. She could tell he was a no-nonsense, business-only type of teacher. He wasn't interested in whether the kids liked him; he'd said as much at Open House night. Carol had been impressed with his course syllabus, though. It would be challenging for Natalie, but she needed a challenge.

"Well, he doesn't know how to teach!" Natalie persisted. "He expects us to basically teach ourselves. He never explains anything. How am I supposed to learn in that class?"

Seeing her daughter's eyes glisten with stubborn tears, Carol wanted to scoop her up and hold her close. But Natalie was 16 now, too old for snuggling on her lap.

"How well did you do on the last test?" Carol asked, already knowing Natalie had gotten a D.

"That's the problem. The tests are nothing like what he goes over in class. I don't know where he gets this stuff!" Natalie paced the room like an anxious cat in a cage. "I want to transfer to another class. I hear Mrs. Sterling actually teaches in her section of this class. I can't afford low grades this year, Mom."

"What about the supplementary study software he gave you? Did you go through that? Did the test have anything on it from that?"

"I started it, but it takes so long to finish. But, yes, a lot of the test came from the software review." Natalie's voice softened. "Why can't he just follow the book like every other teacher?"

The tears finally escaped. Natalie sat on the living-room floor at her mother's feet. "I don't want to have to work this hard," she finally admitted. "Too many Cs and I won't get that full scholarship . . ."

Carol sighed. At least Natalie admitted she didn't want to work that hard; she'd never had to before, and this class scared her to death. Carol knew hitting the wall was an important step for Natalie, but watching her little girl crumble under the pressure was hard for a mother to bear.

Should she intervene or not? Carol wondered whether she should try to get Natalie's schedule changed, or just encourage her to stick it out. Natalie was already halfway through the semester. Yet she couldn't afford any more Cs on her report card if she was going to qualify for the scholarship—the only thing that would make college possible.

All in the Timing

Remember that old Kenny Rogers song "The Gambler"? As we consider the question of when to intercede on behalf of our children, let's adapt the refrain for our purposes:

> You got to know when to stand up,
> Know when to sit down,
> Know when to open your mouth, know when to shut it;
> You never throw a tantrum
> When a kind word makes a difference;
> Wait your turn and just stay focused
> And glorify the Son.

Even if all you have for inspiration is my little ditty, you can see that deciding to stand up for your child is only the first step. For many of us, that step isn't an easy one. Those inclined to jump in with both feet don't fear the leap, but need to look first.

For some parents, choosing to step in is a no-brainer. Why wouldn't they? If your child needs help, you give it—right? But sometimes restraint is the better choice.

How do you decide? Here are seven factors to consider.

1. *Are the stakes low or high?*

Let's say you're facing a choice like Carol's. If I ask you whether it's a low- or high-stakes situation, you might say, "High stakes!"

I challenge you to think about this carefully, though. The truth is that not every dilemma our children find themselves in is a matter of life or death. Often it's more about our comfort than our children's futures.

If the science curriculum at your daughter's school teaches

evolution, for example, it may make you uncomfortable if you believe in creationism or intelligent design. This may or may not mean that your daughter's physical, academic, or spiritual life is in jeopardy. For some children such a situation can be life-changing, while for others it barely registers on their radar—even if all sorts of alarms go off in our own heads.

For some parents, choosing to step in is a no-brainer. But sometimes restraint is the better choice.

Our pasts can teach us a lot about how and why we advocate for our children. If you were bullied as a child, you may be sensitive to any inkling of aggressive behavior toward your children by other kids. If you felt unfairly judged during a competition or tryout, you may find yourself jumping in and demanding fairness for your child.

When we've been mistreated, we want to make sure that doesn't happen to those we love. Understandable as that is, it's not always a reason to step in.

High-stakes situations require immediate attention and action; without intervention, our children may not recover. Low-stakes situations require vigilance and discernment; we need to watch to make sure things don't escalate, that our children can handle themselves and stand on their own.

It's the difference between rushing to catch a child who's falling off the jungle gym—and watching warily as he climbs to the top of the slide by himself. You can go down the slide with him on your lap for only so long. He will outgrow you; he must outgrow you.

Training our children to stand up for themselves starts early. It may begin as you watch your toddler play with a friend, not interfering when one pulls a toy from the other. It may continue as you listen supportively to your daughter as she tells her girlfriend on the phone that she didn't appreciate being talked about behind her back. This is how we learn to discern when to step in.

Ask yourself: Is this a "falling off the jungle gym" situation or a "first time down the slide by himself" situation? You know your child better than anyone else; let that knowledge, not fears and grudges from your own past, guide you.

2. *Is the territory friendly or hostile?*

Deciding to take action isn't something done lightly. It's important to assess the situation first and determine the risks. Are you entering friendly or hostile territory?

Advocacy can feel like a battle. During any military operation, intelligence is gathered about the situation at hand.

I'm not suggesting that you must retreat if you face hostility. But it's important to know what you're up against before deciding on a course of action.

Remember Carol? She knew enough about her daughter's science teacher, Mr. Hayden, to realize that he had no desire to make friends. Being friendly may not be high on his priority list, but that doesn't necessarily mean he's hostile. And it doesn't mean he wouldn't be open to a mutually productive relationship with parents.

What does Carol really know about Mr. Hayden? She encountered him only once at Open House night for about 10 minutes. She mainly knows what her daughter has told her. Teachers have an old saying: "I won't believe everything your kid says about you, if you don't believe everything he says about me." Our intelligence gathering needs to be more thorough than simply listening to our children.

Primary sources are always preferable to secondary ones. It's always more reliable to get information firsthand. If we rely on what other people say about a teacher, doctor, coach, psychologist, social worker, judge, or another child's parent, we risk misjudging that person.

People are always willing to tell you horror stories about their experiences with others. "Don't expect the scoutmaster to call you back; he never does," they warn, or, "The school nurse isn't interested in anything a parent has to say." Their experience doesn't have to be yours. Base your opinions about friendliness and hostility on your own experiences, not someone else's.

3. *Do you want instant or cooked?*

My mother preferred to cook chocolate pudding instead of making the instant kind. The latter would have saved her precious minutes and energy as the mother of five children, but she stood over the stove and patiently stirred the pudding to make sure it didn't scorch on the bottom. The result was a creaminess not to be compared to the quick version, and praises from her family that included, "You're the best mom ever!" To this day, I prefer cooked pudding.

There are advantages to waiting for what you want. Sometimes our children understand that better than we do.

When our oldest son began attending a new charter high school, I was thrilled at first. Eventually, though, I realized there were many experiences he would miss—clubs, sports, band, choir, drama—all things he enjoyed. With only 36 students in his graduating class, social opportunities were limited. And driving him to and from school got old fast, especially when he could be going to the high school I went to across the street.

Getting impatient, I started asking questions—leading questions.

"Don't you want the chance to perform in a school play again?" I said on our way home one day.

"It's no big deal, Mom," Chris said. "I have what I need at this school."

"But you can still change your mind," I pushed. "In fact, you can change your mind even after this school year is done."

"I'm not going to change my mind. I'd rather get two years of college out of the way than play in marching band or go to prom."

"But you'll never get these years back," I said. "I can go to the high school across the street and make sure you can get the classes you want. There's no harm in asking."

"Mom, I'm fine! I'm happy where I am. Don't worry about it. I want to give this school a chance."

I needed to give him time to make things work out the way he wanted, not the way I wanted. I wanted him to have it all, right now. I wanted him to get the college courses he needed *and* have a traditional high school experience.

Sometimes you can get what you want, just not all at the same time.

It's not that we can't buy the sparkly gum at the checkout counter; we just can't have it until after dinner. It's not that we can't ever play on the varsity soccer team; we just have to wait until we qualify. It's not that Natalie can't change her schedule; she just needs to make sure she's doing her best before giving up.

As advocates for our children, we need to determine which will yield the best results: instant or cooked?

4. *Are you volunteer or drafted?*

Perhaps you've got your foot in the air, ready to step up and go to bat for your child. Let's pull that foot back for a moment and consider one more aspect of deciding whether to intervene.

Did you volunteer for this assignment, or were you drafted? Some situations make us sprint into action. Some drag us, kicking and screaming, into the advocacy role. Still others simply prod us to walk obediently into battle like good soldiers. It seems easier to do what you must when you've volunteered for it; otherwise, reluctance and hesitation may cause you to protest, "I didn't sign up for this!"

> *Some situations drag us, kicking and screaming, into the advocacy role.*

Aileen was drafted, but grew into the role. Her son, Michael, was a preemie, designated as such because of his weight, not the timing of his birth. He scored a 5 on his Apgar test, with 10 being the highest possible score, when he was born.

Aileen knew within the first 24 hours that Michael was different from his older sister. It seemed that he never stopped crying; he was difficult to soothe, had a poor sucking reflex, and threw up most of what he ate.

Reluctant to tell friends or family about the daily nightmare she and her husband, Chuck, were living, Aileen struggled in silence. When they went out in public, she had to contend with stares and whispered comments like, "She certainly doesn't have control over her child, does she?"

Aileen felt like a failure as a mother. Chuck, ever the optimist, told her, "Well, this one will make us earn our keep. He's the one who'll make parents of us. The first one was too easy."

Pediatricians said Michael would grow out of it. Relatives said he needed more discipline—or more love.

Once Michael hit school age, teachers said he needed testing. Aileen and Chuck knew only that they needed support—and that all they could find were opponents, naysayers, and bullies.

Aileen researched every possible disease, disorder, and disposition that might be contributing to her son's struggles. She coordinated doctors' appointments, therapists' consultations, and other meetings. Little by little she took on the role of educator when the schools threw up their hands in defeat.

She became Michael's cheerleader. Frustration and love forced her into unfamiliar territory every day as she stood up for him. There was no other way; autism, even in its mildest form, was not well documented in those days.

If you're planning to intervene only to placate someone else, your reluctance may make you a less effective advocate. Is that "someone else" willing to do the job? If you're "it," pray for the kind of strength Aileen found. As her story shows, even draftees can become volunteers.

5. *Is it urgent or timeless?*

Is there an "expiration date" on the situation you face? If you don't act now, will a crucial opportunity be lost? Will the issue be rendered moot by the passage of time?

Some problems seem more urgent than they really are; our emotions may demand revenge, closure, or a return to "normalcy." But others are truly time-sensitive. Some examples:

- Your child's health is threatened by an apparent misdiagnosis.
- A literal deadline (scholarship application, court date, credit card payment, awards banquet, semester's end) is looming.
- Delaying action will make success harder to achieve later (for instance, your child will fall further behind in that algebra class).

- The person best able to help you now will be unavailable
  in the future.

If we wait too long to step in, we may miss the window of
opportunity. This is where urgency sometimes takes precedence
over other important concerns. And since some of us tend to
procrastinate, it's vital that when we decide to act that we do so
immediately.

6. *Are you alone or partnered?*

When I was a child, I liked using the seesaw at the playground. Sometimes I had my younger brother sit with me on my
side in order to counterbalance my big brute of an older cousin
on the other.

Advocacy can be the same way. If you're a "lightweight" facing a "heavyweight," you may need to compensate by adding
someone to your side. When deciding whether to intervene, ask
whether you have that person.

That was the case with Val. The mother of a boy named
Joshua, she seemed to be up against a Goliath. Joshua had been
classified as having Attention Deficit/Hyperactivity Disorder
with sensory integration problems. He began to exhibit symptoms of selective mutism, then became aggressive and began to
hit other children.

When Joshua was placed in a new environment that supposedly catered to children with his diagnosis, Val grew concerned
that he was learning the wrong behaviors. She met with the
principal and the teacher at this school, but felt her insights
were dismissed. She felt small, and that her opinions carried no
weight.

Instead of getting off the seesaw, she decided to invite me
along for the ride. All I did was counsel her about the workings

of the school and how it did or didn't match her son's needs. She just needed confirmation that her opinions were valid; in her mind, that gave her the stature to stand up for Joshua.

No matter what weight class you think the experts compete in, how you perceive your own weight is what makes the difference. If you see yourself as a lightweight, bring someone with you to balance the seesaw—or gain the expertise necessary to compete in this weight class. Either way can get you ready.

7. Are you nagging or not?

Most teachers, coaches, doctors, and the like say that parents nag and complain too much. When considering whether to intervene, ask yourself whether you've already addressed the issue at hand—and whether you need to wait for a response or take a different tack.

My mother used to say that if she asked my dad more than three times to take care of something, it became nagging. So she stopped at three requests. Do we realize that our intervention turns to nagging when we ask a coach over and over again to let our son play right field, or when we repeatedly ask our mother-in-law to stop giving the kids soda when they eat at her house? If what we say seems to "go in one ear and out the other," it probably does.

Pushing our opinion on how we think someone else should do his job is usually ineffective and borders on harassment. I may not *feel* I'm dishonoring my son's coach's position when I continually remind him that Chris hasn't had a chance to play right field yet, but he may hear it that way.

When we nag, those we target shut down. We're no longer helping our children get what they need; we're hurting all parties concerned, and it's time to take a step back.

When Standing Up Is Scary

Opposition affects people differently. Parents who choose not to assert their rights and those of their children do so for many different reasons. These fears are often justified—and difficult to combat.

You may find it difficult to stand tall when . . .

- You've been isolated or excluded by others who were supposed to be on your side. If you seem to be the only parent with this complaint, and others distance themselves from you because of it, you may back down.
- You fear losing your job or reputation if you stand up for your child. Are you willing to take that risk? Only you can answer that question.
- You fear being seen as a troublemaker or "nightmare parent." This can be a real consequence of standing up for your child, but this book is intended to help you avoid it.
- Everyone else denies there's a problem and accuses you of lying.
- You're reluctant to complain about a fellow human being—especially a Christian. Ask yourself whether you've been sinned against, or are being pressured to sin. Have you approached the "other side" privately, or are you leaping prematurely to a more public forum?
- Those in charge protect your opponent, even though they know he or she is in the wrong. It feels like a no-win situation for you.
- Your opponent feigns being a victim and manipulates your sympathies. Consider your behavior carefully, proceeding only when you can say honestly that you didn't victimize him or her.

Reasons like these can be paralyzing. Examine your motivations and behavior, asking God to search your heart for any deceit. Be honest with yourself and seek counsel from a pastor or other mature believer before charging into a situation and making a stand.

The Rest of the Story

When we first met Carol, she was trying to choose whether or not to jump in and help her daughter, Natalie, get what she thought she needed from her advanced chemistry class. Here's what happened.

Carol decided she should hear Mr. Hayden's side of the story before reacting to Natalie's request to change her class schedule. She found the teacher surprisingly responsive to her e-mails.

Mr. Hayden encouraged her to let Natalie remain in his classroom, believing she wouldn't be challenged enough in the other section of the class. "Your daughter has a future in the sciences if she wants one," he explained. "I can offer her the discipline and attention to detail she'll need in order to be successful in her college-level science courses."

Startled that Mr. Hayden had such insight into her daughter's strengths and interests, Carol told Natalie that staying put was the best decision for now.

"But I don't know how to do better in his class," the girl complained. "He never tells us anything. It's like a secret or something."

"All you have to do is ask him the question every teacher is dying to hear," Carol replied. " 'What can I do to succeed in this class?' You'd be surprised how few students ask. It will be like music to Mr. Hayden's ears!"

"And if it doesn't work, can you get me switched out then?" Natalie asked.

"No, I think you can handle this one on your own. You have my support and my prayers, and you have a teacher willing to help you succeed. So I suggest you give it your best shot. Handle this one, and when you're in college you'll be able to handle any professor they throw at you."

Kissing her daughter on the head as she'd done when Natalie was a little girl, Carol prayed for the best.

When to Sit Down

As Carol found, stepping into the ring on your child's behalf isn't always the best solution. Here are some things to remember about knowing when to sit down instead.

1. *Our attempts to "help" don't always go over well with our children.* The older they get, the more they'd prefer we "stay out of it."

Sometimes letting kids fail in a safe environment is the best way to stand up for their long-term success.

If you can safely leave the standing up to your kids, give it a try. It's guaranteed to be a stretching experience for everyone involved.

2. *Don't intervene to protect children from all the consequences of their actions.* Learning from mistakes is a time-honored way to grow. The child who's always "bailed out"—whether from jail or from forgetting to write a book report—won't get acquainted with responsibility, self-discipline, or respecting authority.

It takes wisdom, courage, and sometimes the help of professionals to know whether "rescuing" a child is a good idea. You don't want to endanger your child. But when "helping" becomes enabling, there's a problem. Sometimes letting kids fail in a safe environment is the best way to stand up for their long-term success.

Here's how one mom discovered this principle.

I knew my daughter needed to take the initiative and responsibility for her own education. However, relying on her own initiative and responsibility resulted in the possibility of her failing three classes. We talked, talked, and talked some more, fought, met with teachers, counselors, and basically had major drama for months on end as I tried to "help."

In the end she failed one class and repeated it in the summer. I think this had more impact than all the talking, meeting, arguing, and "helping" I did. She missed her favorite summer activity because she had to go to summer school.

I'm glad to say that the natural consequences of her actions appear to have changed her attitude about school and what it is going to take to succeed. She now has a tutor in her most difficult subject and knows that I, and a myriad of friends, are here to help should she require it, but the work itself and the monitoring of its completion is her job. Asking for help is also her responsibility.

I'll ask how it's going. If the response I get is, "Fine," I'm going to believe it and back off. If help is asked for, it will be provided. It has been very difficult for me to back off, and yet it appears to be working.

I learned the hard way that it is up to her, and that she'll learn much more quickly from the results of her actions than she will from advice and "hand-holding." She'll find her way, even if she screws up occasionally along the way.

My advice? Let her stand on her own, but let her know you're there if she needs you.

3. *Don't be a helicopter.* Children born between 1980 and 2000 are sometimes called "Millennials." Their parents have been labeled "Helicopter Parents." In other words, they hover. They're considered a little too involved in their children's lives.

Some school officials have discovered that parents call their kids' cell phones at school as often as friends do. Text messaging from parents to kids is becoming more frequent. According to the dean's offices at the University of Florida, University of South Florida, and Florida State University, parents of college students are doing things like these:

- Attending orientation with their freshmen, as if the parents are the ones going to college.
- Staying with kids the first week of classes to make sure they're okay.
- Logging on to their kids' personal school Web accounts to check grades, then calling the dean when they don't like what they see.
- Calling administrators to complain when kids don't get into the courses they want.
- Keeping in constant touch via cell phone and e-mail, and even calling to wake kids up to make sure they get to their 8:00 A.M. classes.
- Haggling with job recruiters to make sure their seniors get the "right" job.[1]

Reports of writing kids' term papers for them and intervening in roommate disputes are beginning to surface. Even though parents mean well, they're creating a generation of dependent child-adults.

4. *Sometimes you have no choice.* There are times when stepping back is the only real option—simply because some people and situations won't budge no matter how hard you push.

Forcing issues to the point of damaging a relationship or your credibility as a person of faith isn't worth it. Before that happens, remember a wiser course—praying for a resolution of the problem.

Trust and Obey

Knowing "when to hold 'em" and "when to fold 'em" isn't always simple. There are times when fervently pursuing a quality experience for our children leads in a positive direction. But there are times when we need to step back and trust that God has our children's lives in His hands.

Sometimes, sitting at the playground and watching our little ones interact in the sandbox, we need to let them work out their tiffs, stepping in only when absolutely necessary. We can pray for them to have open hearts, open minds, and discerning spirits. We can pray for their safety and the strength to stand up for themselves.

And when playgrounds and sandboxes become after-school jobs and driver's education, we can do the same.

Our job is to train our kids, not live their lives for them. "Teach a youth about the way he should go; even when he is old he will not depart from it" (Proverbs 22:6, HCSB).

This is really all we're expected to do—and it's a challenging task indeed.

6

A MATCH MADE IN HEAVEN

Guiding Principle #4:
*Make sure your words and actions
are in harmony when dealing with others.*

Kitty believes in the values learned from playing team sports—sportsmanship, teamwork, and discipline. That's why she makes sure her children are always playing on a team.

This year her ten-year-old, Kevin, played baseball. "It started out in the usual way at the beginning of the season," Kitty explains. "Everyone got a chance to play the position they tried out for and were selected to play. Kevin was good at pitching, but not very good at catching the ball. Everyone has their strengths and weaknesses."

But soon it was clear that Kevin wasn't going to spend much time as a pitcher. Finally Kitty took him to see the league manager.

"When the team came together after a few practices," Kitty explained, "Kevin was on the list as a pitcher, along with two other boys. One of the other boys was the coach's son."

"That's not unusual," the manager said. "That's the reason some parents choose to coach at all—to be where their kids play."

"I understand," Kitty said. "But after a few games a pattern emerged. No matter who started pitching a game, after the other team got a hit, that pitcher was removed and the coach's son was put on the mound."

"I'm assuming that's because he's the better pitcher. A strategic move on the coach's part," the manager said. "What's your complaint, Mrs. Simpson? So far I haven't heard anything out of bounds."

Kitty sat up straighter in her chair and made eye contact with the manager. "All the parents noticed this favoritism, sir. Several of us asked the coach if he didn't think he should manage the pitching rotation more equitably. He always mouthed agreement, but he never changed."

There, she thought. *I said it.*

"So basically, you all ganged up on the coach and challenged his authority," the manager said. "This coach has a stellar reputation. Everyone wants to be on his team because he creates winners." The manager paused. "If I were the coach, I'd be in here complaining about *you*."

Kitty couldn't believe her ears. *Even this guy doesn't get it.*

"Mr. Jameson, this isn't about winning," she said. "It's about giving these boys a quality experience. I just wanted my son and the other boys to have a chance to experience the game and enjoy being part of a team. I felt that what all the boys needed at this time is coaching to develop their skills, encouragement to do their best, and inspiration to love the game itself. What they didn't need was to feel that they'd failed anyone if they didn't win."

"Well, those are great sentiments," the manager said. "But that's not what this league is about. This is competitive ball, Mrs. Simpson, not a developmental league. We're here to win games—not scatter trophies like birdseed so everyone feels good about himself."

Kitty and Kevin sat there, speechless. At length she thanked Mr. Jameson for his time.

Then, on the way out, she left Kevin's uniform on the manager's desk.

Mr. Jameson wasn't surprised. He'd heard it all before.

Just one more parent who doesn't get it, he thought.

Why did Kitty have her son quit the team? Because she believed her expectations for this sports experience had been violated. Whether or not she chose the best course, one thing is certain: She had to do *something* in order to be true to what she felt was right.

She chose to walk away. That's not the only possibility. We'll look at others in this chapter. We'll also examine what to do when we're tempted to stand up for our kids in ways that aren't true to our stated values.

In other words, we're about to consider what happens in advocacy when our beliefs and actions don't match.

The Dissonance Dilemma

Life is full of contradictions. Once in a while, that creates a real problem.

Whether we ever say them out loud or not, we operate on a set of values and principles. Usually our behavior is an extension of those beliefs. When what we say we believe and what we do aren't the same, there's disharmony, tension, stress.

This conflict is *dissonance*. It happens in our marriages, jobs, friendships—and with anyone connected to our children. When we see others' actions failing to match their words, we may accuse them of being hypocrites. When we fail to turn our beliefs into deeds, we may level the same accusation against ourselves—or feel like cowards.

In Kitty's mind, she would have been a hypocrite if she'd continued to accept the situation on Kevin's baseball team. She already saw the coach and manager as hypocrites themselves, failing to live up to the values she assumed they held. Once that happened, the relationship soured and any attempts at advocacy appeared pointless.

Dealing with differences between words and deeds is a must when we're standing up for our kids. Ignoring the issue endangers the whole advocacy process.

When Others Aren't Consistent

Often we find ourselves in the advocacy arena because promises were broken. Service providers or authority figures tell us one thing and then do another, or they don't tell us "the whole truth" and we feel ambushed.

We need to be vigilant to make sure that what people do matches what they said they would do. That's not being nitpicky; it's being a good parent.

Julie's 15-year-old son is in special education at their local high school. Once in a while he's mainstreamed into the regular classroom. In ninth grade Julie permitted him to be mainstreamed into a health education class that focused on human sexuality.

Before making that decision, Julie examined the curriculum the teacher said would be used in the class. As a person with a Christian worldview, Julie wanted to make sure the course didn't contradict that view. From what she could tell, this would be an appropriate class for John at this point in his life; the textbook appeared to include only facts, not opinion.

But one day John came home, telling a tale Julie couldn't believe.

"Our teacher said that AIDS came from shepherds having intercourse with their sheep," he said matter-of-factly. "She said they did this many years ago when they were shepherding, to release their sexual energy. I didn't know that's where it came from, Mom."

Julie's anger could have blown off the top of Mount McKinley! She couldn't ignore this lie, or the fact that the teacher had crossed the line of appropriate behavior by telling it. Giving a false explanation for the origin of AIDS to impressionable children was a breach of trust in Julie's mind.

"I was angry for several reasons," Julie explained later, "but I focused on one: This was not in the curriculum! I knew that trying to get my point across on any moral basis would obviously go unnoticed."

Julie believed that the broken promise to stick with the curriculum required drastic measures. She started with the homeroom teacher to formally issue her complaint. He recommended that she go to the principal, who made sure the teacher in question called Julie. That conversation didn't go very well.

"I was able to get her to back down on her stance and apologize," Julie explained. "But I wasn't able to change her mind about the appropriateness of that comment."

Julie wanted the teacher fired, or at least removed from teaching the class. But she didn't get what she wanted. Asked how she felt about the outcome, Julie said she felt satisfied that her message was received, but not about how things ultimately played out.

There are no guarantees of success when we stand up for our kids. We can't control how other people behave.

But we can control ourselves. Make sure *your* words are consistent with *your* actions. Don't be the promise breaker.

When We Aren't Consistent

I learned a lot from my mother about parenting. I often went to her for advice when I faced an obstacle to our desired quality of life.

When the playground bully tripped my son yet again, I called Mom. When a good friend wouldn't tell her daughter to "play nicely" or give "soft touches" to our toddler, I asked, "What do I do? How do I handle this?"

Mom always had great advice. I knew I could trust what she said because I remembered how she'd handled these problems when we were growing up.

Some of us, though, don't always follow the advice that comes out of our mouths. There's the two-pack-a-day smoker who tells his son not to smoke because the Surgeon General says it's bad. Or the nutritionist who feeds her kids junk food because it's what they want.

There's also the parent who claims biblical values, but approaches advocacy as if the end justifies the means—any means.

Sometimes when we feel the odds are against us, we look for any strategy that might give us an advantage. Some are clever; others are questionable at best. Flirting with the latter can work against your integrity—and your cause.

> Make sure your integrity doesn't find itself on the altar.

Do you find yourself saying, "I'll do whatever it takes to get my child's needs met"? These are the words of a dedicated parent, but it's important to set boundaries. It's fine to be willing to sacrifice on behalf of our children, but we need to make sure our integrity doesn't find itself on the altar as well.

Let's shine a light on some shadowy stand-up practices:

- The Workaround—bypassing the authority who stands in our way
- Secret Identities—pretending we have "friends in high places" who'll overrule or punish the person we're dealing with
- Burying Information—conveniently misplacing e-mails, notes, forms, or other evidence needed by decision makers
- Claiming Ignorance—deflecting judgment by saying, "I didn't realize," or "No one told me," or "I wish I'd known," when you really *did* know.

Why do we do these things? Usually it's to avoid a confrontation or to bolster a weak case. Maybe we're trying to buy ourselves and our kids more time. But ready or not, we need to stay in the light when we act on behalf of our children.

Jesus did what it took to get our need for salvation met—and He did it in the light. He sacrificed His life to stand in the gap for us. Tempted to find a way around the crucifixion when He prayed to God the Father in the Garden of Gethsemane, He chose to do things God's way. He didn't try to find an escape route under cover of darkness. He could have denied who He was when the soldiers came for Him that night, but stepped forward into the light of their torches.

Getting our children what they want or what we think they need at the cost of our integrity leaves a legacy of regret. Think about how Rebekah in the Bible used deception to steal Isaac's blessing for their son Jacob (Genesis 27). When Jacob pretended to the blind Isaac that he was brother Esau, Rebekah got what she wanted for him. Jacob, on the other hand, got a life of struggle that made him wait for the fulfillment of God's promises longer than he should have.

To get our children what they need in the long run, we have to step back in the short term—and do things God's way.

The Rules of Engagement

So what is "God's way" of standing up for your child? To answer that question, it may help to look at what are sometimes called "rules of engagement."

That's a military term—fitting, since it often feels like we're at war when we stand in the gap for our children. But every organization has such rules, though they're not always posted where anyone can see them. Parents with faith-based values need to ask what kinds of negotiations are likely to succeed—and let us leave with our integrity intact.

Rose is one parent who's had to consider how to fight the battles she faces. She struggles to this day to get her son's academic needs met. Though he was diagnosed with Sensory Integration Disorder (SID), his teachers didn't take that into account when they dealt with him in the classroom.

"They kept telling us how bad he was doing in school, yet they would say in the same breath that he was highly intelligent," Rose explains. "They ended up sending him to a program for mentally disturbed children. It was only a temporary program [45 days], since he isn't mentally disturbed."

Rose learned this was the "normal" procedure at that school to determine the course of action for her son. "The program is directed to gathering information on what can help the child succeed in the classroom. They did come up with some great ways to help. By law the school then has to comply. Well, they didn't."

Rose finally took her son out of the public school and started homeschooling. The law was on her side, but she chose not to use legal action to get her son's needs met.

Did Rose do the right thing?

In the military, rules of engagement govern the use of force—when, where, against whom, and how it may be employed. Let's look at how those concepts might apply to standing up for our children without throwing our beliefs overboard.

1. *When may force be used?*

For parents with a biblical worldview, the rules of engagement are founded on biblical principles. Interpretations differ over whether believers should use "force" in the usual sense; so, for our purposes, let's limit our discussion to one kind of force—the powerful declaration of truth. Ephesians 4:15 urges us to speak the truth in love. When those involved in caring for our children promote a distorted version of the truth or outright lies, it's our duty to speak the truth lovingly. Sometimes it requires us to "set the record straight."

That's what Rose did. She forced the truth to the surface. She also did it admirably, speaking the truth directly to the teachers—not behind their backs.

2. Where may force be used?

Those of us with Bully tendencies may be tempted to march uninvited into a volunteer coach's place of employment and confront him with a truth that's been denied or distorted. Those of us with Buddy tendencies may be tempted to talk to everyone *except* the youth pastor who needs to hear the truth from us, whether as a "prayer request" at a Bible study or in an Internet blog. Neither is appropriate.

> Our goal in confronting with the truth should not be to humiliate, slander, or discredit.

When Superintendent Clayton Wilcox of Pinellas County Schools in Florida began to write regularly on a blog hosted by the *St. Petersburg Times*, some parents misused it. Issuing a call to arms, they conducted an online filibuster against some of the superintendent's decisions by filling up the blog with "noise." It was not the right place or the right response.

Our goal in confronting with the truth should not be to humiliate, slander, or discredit. And the venue should match the issue. If this is a private and personal conflict, choose a private and personal space for confrontation. If it affects hundreds or thousands of children battling the same issue, and personal confrontation hasn't helped, a public forum may be appropriate.

3. *Against whom may force be used?*

You can speak the truth in love to anyone, but you'll be wasting your time if the person isn't sympathetic or doesn't have the power to act on your complaint. Rose knew school staff members were not willing to comply with the law, so the truth would fall on deaf ears. Even though their behavior was disappointing and illegal, Rose took her son elsewhere.

The truth is precious; choose carefully to whom you offer it on your child's behalf.

4. *How may force be used?*

Once you find the right person and setting, consider how to speak your truth. Anger, even if it's your weapon of choice, doesn't make the unwilling willing or the deaf able to hear. The truth should be spoken in love. If we engage in heated arguments, hair-splitting semantics, or disrespectful accusations, we have no one to blame but ourselves if the truth doesn't arise from the muck.

As I've written elsewhere, our tone communicates our real message. In fact, the message can easily be drowned out by our attitude.

"I lost my cool and they stopped listening," Chip admitted after one verbal battle. "They weren't going to hear a word I said about our son at this point." This is where many parents lose the "war."

How shall we then speak the truth? The apostle Paul offers this advice: "Let your speech always be filled with grace, as though seasoned with salt, so that you will know how you should respond to each person" (Colossians 4:6).

Making the Match

Following the right rules of engagement can go a long way toward dialing down dissonance. But sometimes the conflict comes from outside sources—a family member who tries to control the way we parent, a boss whose expectations of his teenage workers are too high, a drama director who requires anyone cast in a play to use the profanity in the script.

How can we reduce or eliminate the tension we feel when what we believe doesn't match what we "have" to do? Here are three commonly used methods.

1. *Make the conflict unimportant.*

Let's say you've enrolled your child in a prestigious, expensive private school. Soon you discover that it doesn't address your child's newly diagnosed learning disability.

Now there's dissonance—disharmony—between your discovery and your belief that this is a high-quality school that should meet your child's learning needs. You're squirming in your seat, uncomfortable with the fact that your son won't be able to get his needs met here. This discomfort forces change; you have a decision to make.

One way to reduce the tension in this situation is to decide that it doesn't really matter—since the school also has a great art program and your son excels in this area. You're reducing the importance of your beliefs—about the school and your son's learning needs. You decide to let him remain at the school.

2. *Change your belief.*

Another way to deal with dissonance is to adhere to a new belief that changes the balance. Maybe you decide that since the student-to-teacher ratio is only 10 to 1, there's a good chance your son's needs will be met even if there's no formal program in place. You conclude that this new information balances things out. You keep your son at the school.

One cautionary note about adjusting your beliefs: Be brutally honest with yourself about what you've decided to believe. Sometimes we tell ourselves what we want to hear in order to avoid a confrontation or "make everything okay" when it really isn't.

3. *Change your behavior.*

Let's say you're not willing to discount your son's learning needs or make the school out to be something it's not in order to "feel better" about the situation. If you're unable or unwilling to change what you believe—or its importance—to match your behavior, your only other choice is to change your actions.

As a result, you pull your son out of the private school and make another choice.

Changing your behavior is the most difficult solution for many of

> Sometimes we tell ourselves what we want to hear in order to avoid a confrontation or "make everything okay."

us. It means admitting that your first choice probably wasn't the right one. It can be humbling, even humiliating. Sometimes it even costs money!

In the case of the private school, there's a good chance you had your child on a waiting list for a long time, rearranged your life to drive him to and from this school, bought uniforms, and paid tuition up front. You'll have to explain to the principal why you're withdrawing your child. You may have to put up with a critical mother-in-law and judgmental friends, all of whom think you're making a big mistake.

How It Really Works

Parents usually don't just pick one of the three aforementioned alternatives and run with it. It's common to start by trying to reduce the importance of the dissonance; if that doesn't work, many people attempt to adjust their beliefs. Finally, when they can't stand it anymore, they change their actions to honestly reflect their convictions.

Our family went through this process when our children reached school age. As a teacher myself, I didn't hesitate to place our kids in our neighborhood public school. Unfortunately, by the time our oldest reached the end of kindergarten, I realized that this school was unable or unwilling to meet his needs as a gifted learner. Uncomfortable with this insight, I began to look for ways to "make it better."

First I tried making the conflict unimportant. I told myself and my son that things would improve. I told him he had to learn that being bored was part of life; I told myself I needed to learn there was no such thing as a perfect school. This thinking held us for a while, kind of like holding a piece of tissue on a cut. Not surprisingly, the problem bled right through.

Next, I tried to change my beliefs. As Christopher grew more frustrated in his attempts at "learning how to be bored," I decided we should concentrate on what the school *did* offer him. I enrolled him in the once-a-week gifted program. But he began to shut down in his regular class. The tension was so thick that it began to choke the joy out of our lives.

By the middle of second grade, Christopher and the school had seen enough of each other. I didn't want to give up; I wanted to find a way to make this work. But when my son stopped trying and complained daily about stomachaches, I had to change my behavior. We pulled him out of public school, and I home-schooled him for the rest of his elementary school years.

Working Toward Harmony

When you battle on behalf of your child, you don't always win. But that doesn't mean the hope for harmony is lost. Harmony is more than successful negotiation; it results when you behave in a way that truly reflects what you believe.

If you care about following the example of Jesus, it's even more important to work toward harmony. As you negotiate, you don't want to cross over into nagging. As you battle, you don't want to end up belittling.

Our reputations as believers are at stake during these encounters. Our behavior reflects not only on our faith, but on the God we say we believe in.

Some people are always on the hunt for contradiction in Christians. I've heard teachers in the lounge comment, "Sarah's parents go to my church. You'd never know they were believers by the way they acted in my classroom the other day." And, "I hear she takes her kids to church twice a week. Seems to me they should be going even more!"

"Walk in a manner worthy of the God who calls you into His own kingdom and glory" (1 Thessalonians 2:12). When the coach, doctor, or teacher breaks a promise, make sure you approach him or her in a way that reflects who you are and what you believe. Walk worthy of your calling as a parent and as a child of God—and remember that He isn't the only One who's watching.

7

ASKING FOR DIRECTIONS

It's better to know some of the questions than all of the answers.
—JAMES THURBER

Guiding Principle #5:
*Be willing to seek advice when you're unsure,
instead of pretending you know it all.*

D on't you hate it when men refuse to ask for directions when it's obvious that they're lost?

No offense, guys, but it drives us girls nuts! Why waste time, energy, and gas driving around pretending things looks familiar when you have no clue how to get where you want to go?

Then again, I do the same thing. As a teacher, I tend to feel pretty secure about solving my children's school-related problems. Normally I know who to go to and what to ask to get the job done. I don't pretend to know much about my kids' health care or their sports involvement, but I do know school.

Yet I've been blindsided on more than one occasion.

When our youngest son, Charles, was in the sixth grade, he had an accident six weeks before the end of the year. Falling during recess, he broke his wrist in five places and dislocated it. It was a horrendous break.

During the first week he stayed home, heavily medicated for pain and unable to use his right hand at all (he's right-handed). I went to the school, letting teachers know what was going on. I asked them to tell me upon his return the following week how they would help our son complete his work for the remainder of the year.

When we sent Charles back to school with a cast and half of his pain medication, a number of his teachers penalized him for not turning in work he'd missed the week before. Worse, when I met with all six of his teachers in a group conference, I discovered they had made no plan to help Charles.

"I guess Charles is going to have a hard time completing the work for the remainder of the year," one teacher said. None of the teachers had any suggestions. Any ideas that my husband and I offered were dismissed.

We decided to pull Charles out of school for the next five weeks and homeschool him. When the school superintendent got wind of our decision, he asked to see us in his office.

He said he was very surprised that the school hadn't offered to invoke Section 504 to help Charles. I had no idea what Section 504 was.

It turns out that Section 504 of the Rehabilitation Act requires a school district to provide a "free appropriate public education" to each qualified student with a disability in the district's jurisdiction, regardless of the nature or severity of the disability. A "temporary 504" can be invoked when a child is hospitalized or has an injury that gets in the way of his learning.

Charles' shattered wrist certainly qualified. But we hadn't known it was something we could ask for.

Roll Down the Window

If we don't ask for what our children need, we probably won't get it. And no matter how well prepared we think we are to stand up for our kids, there will always be gaps in our understanding.

So far I've built you up to believe that you are your child's best advocate. Without question, you're the expert on your child. Still, there will be moments that baffle you. You know your child better than most professionals can, but you also may need help handling his or her unique situation.

If you have a strong Type A personality, you may have to humble yourself to admit you don't know it all. If you lack confidence, you may have to learn to open your mouth and spring those questions you've been afraid to ask.

Jesus told us to ask and we would receive (Matthew 7:7-8). That includes help in standing up for our children. Sometimes God points us in the right direction to get answers; other times we already know which human experts to query. Either way we need to be willing to roll down the window and ask for directions.

No Know-it-alls

Anna and her husband have four children. When their youngest, Jenny, was two years old, they went away for the weekend as a family. Jenny became listless, just lying around most of the time.

Anna knew this was unusual for any two-year-old, especially Jenny. Soon the little girl was running a fever; in Anna's words, "She just didn't look right."

On the two-hour drive home, Jenny looked worse. Anna decided to take her straight to the hospital emergency room instead of waiting for a doctor's appointment the next day.

"When we arrived at the hospital and finally got to see the doctor, I got the 'first-time mothers often overreact' speech. I assured the doctor that I wasn't overreacting and that something was wrong. Two hours later we were sent home and told she might have an upper respiratory infection coming on—and to call our pediatrician the next day. Thirty minutes after we arrived home, Jenny had a *grand mal* seizure and we rushed her back to the same hospital. Her temperature had now shot up to 106.8 degrees!"

Anna didn't trust the emergency room doctor's assessment of her daughter's condition. But she didn't know what questions to ask to get Jenny the help she desperately needed.

"I was asked to leave the room because what they would have to do might be frightening. I refused to leave and assured them that nothing I would see could be worse than the seizure I'd just witnessed."

When all was said and done, the doctors determined that Jenny had a severe bladder infection. She ended up having to take phenobarbital for the next four years.

"From that point on I've become more insistent when it comes to my kids' health care," Anna said.

That was how Anna learned to ask questions.

Whether your child's needs are temporary or permanent, you may find yourself thrown into the questioner's role as Anna was. You might be working for changes in federal or state law or talking to your child's "team" about his or her education; either way, you're unlikely to know in the beginning all you need to know.

Little Jenny, for example, required a champion once she reached school age. She was taking phenobarbital, a controlled substance that must be administered by school personnel during the school day. Her teacher probably had to be told of her chronic bladder infections and the side effects her medication might have. To stand up for Jenny, Anna had to stay one step ahead by asking questions.

> You're unlikely to know in the beginning all you need to know.

Jenny's disability was temporary, but many parents fight lifelong battles due to their children's more permanent challenges. Seldom are they prepared. They didn't take a prenatal "How to Parent a Disabled Child" class. Now it seems all they have are questions.

Detective Work

Andrea didn't believe that her daughter, whom she adopted from a Russian orphanage, would ever grow out of her developmental delays. Even though this child was hers "by choice," not birth, Andrea knew her better than any doctor. And she knew something was terribly wrong.

> My daughter was extremely small for her age. I was told that with proper nourishment she would catch up. She was generally nonresponsive to us. It was more than not knowing our language.
>
> We were told by doctors that her fine motor skills were lacking due to early deprivation, and that proper nutrition

and love would fix the problem. We pointed to Russian medical reports identifying learning disabilities. The doctors told us that they didn't put a lot of stock in an orphanage medical report.

We stayed involved with a network of families who had adopted from Russian orphanages, and we knew some parents whose children even came from the same orphanage as our daughter. Our struggles were similar.

I had read about Attachment Disorder and fetal alcohol exposure. I had also spoken with someone involved in the foster care system and learned that we were experiencing symptoms commonly found in foster children who were in the system because of mothers who were drug addicts. I learned that being underweight, lack of focus, language difficulties, and other developmental delays were typical of children with fetal alcohol or drug exposure. They were not issues that could be outgrown, solved with proper nourishment, or "loved out."

What happened next?

"I kept going to different doctors until one identified the obvious symptoms of Fetal Alcohol Syndrome," Andrea explains.

Andrea's knowledge came from asking question after question until she found the cause of her daughter's condition. She didn't stop because the answers were hard to find or the experts weren't willing to give them. She pressed on in spite of those who were charged with her daughter's care.

Regardless of whether your child exhibits a known or unknown problem, the necessity of gathering information can't be overemphasized. Allison and Rick Martin offer this insight on their Web site, Prematurity.org: "All parents must play detective at times. They must search for clues to keep up with the mysterious changes children can go through in each developmental stage. . . . Each child is unique, and parent detectives may need to evaluate additional information, issues, and referrals from doctors, specialists, therapists, and support groups to identify individual problems and treatment."[1]

Three Kinds of Questions

As detectives, we need to ask three types of questions.

1. *Questions for clarification.* Sometimes we'll have trouble understanding service providers or caregivers. We may not know the "language" used in this new "land," and could use an interpreter.

If we don't ask for help, our credibility could be compromised; we might miss pertinent information. Experts' use of "educationese," "doctor-speak," or "jock talk" could place us in a defensive position.

When Chip and I went to Italy, we learned a very important phrase: "*Mi spiace, non parlo Italiano.*" It means, "I'm sorry, I do not speak Italian." When we said that, the locals went out of their way to speak the little English they knew or find a way that we could communicate through gestures or drawing. This surprised me; I'd expected that once we revealed we couldn't speak their language, some people would take advantage of us. Instead, they worked harder to be understood and to understand.

In the worlds of education or medicine or sports, the experts may not be as accommodating as our Italian friends. They may seem to know secret codes to which they're not in a hurry to offer a key. Sometimes this is done to keep us off balance and out of the loop, or to "puff up" and show "power." Often, though, it's just that specialists spend so much of their time talking to other teachers, medical personnel, or sports enthusiasts that they've forgotten to dial it down when they talk to someone on the "outside."

Don't let language be a barrier to advocacy. Just admit that you don't know what an IEP (Individualized Education Plan), FUO (Fever of Unknown Origin), or bogey (a score of one over par on a hole in golf) is. Humble yourself; take off the mask of the "got it all under control" parent, and say, "Please explain what that means." If needed, enlist the help of a friend on the "inside"—a nurse or retired teacher, for instance—who can translate for you.

> Just admit that you don't know what an IEP, FUO, or bogey is.

2. *Questions that provoke thought.* Provocative questions demand attention and careful consideration. They tend to put your agenda—and your opponent's—in plain view.

Jesus asked provocative questions. Consider when He asked Peter, who had betrayed Him, "Simon, son of John, do you love Me more than these?" (John 21:15)

Let's say your child isn't getting enough game time in his recreational soccer league. You've spoken with the coach about it more than once, but nothing seems to change. You go to the league director and begin with a statement of what you know about the organization: "The core values of the league have always driven every recreational sport you sponsor. It's why we chose it instead of a city-run league."

You follow this up with a statement about a trend you've researched: "I realize that there's been a trend to use volunteers and not staff as soccer coaches lately. But from what I've been told, the volunteers are trained in these core values as well."

Then come the provocative questions: "Are you comfortable with the fact that my son's coach dismisses these core values in favor of competition and excludes players? How does this help instill your core values into kids? What problems do you see in your volunteer training process that might cause this to happen?"

These questions probe. Your opponent will have to seriously consider them before uttering an answer.

3. *Questions to enlist help.* Parents aren't the only ones who stand up for kids. Teachers work every day to make a difference in the life of your child; doctors are available day and night to treat a sick or injured child; coaches sacrifice time with their families to spend time with yours. It's tempting to look at service providers as "them" or the enemy, but far better to form alliances with these important people in your child's life if you can.

The beginning of a relationship is a good time to establish rapport. Ask personal or family-related questions that show genuine interest. If you know your son's teacher is a parent, ask how old his children are and where they go to school. One question leads to another, and over time you may develop a sincere friendship. You may even discover that you have more than your child's welfare in common.

When you need help getting your child's needs met, it's time to ask more questions of your new ally. These might include queries like the following:

- *Is this situation considered common? How is it normally handled here?* When something happens to our child that makes us anxious or ready to fight, we forget that, for service providers, this may seem like just another day. For example, when my obstetrician announced that my son was "breech," he said it as offhandedly as I might say to my husband, "Oh, and pick up some milk on your way home." To the doctor, this was a common occurrence; for me, it was devastating news. To gain perspective, it's crucial that we find out how serious service providers think the situation is.

- *Is the teacher/doctor/coach I'm dealing with open to different points of view?* If you're negotiating with someone other than your "friend on the inside," find out whether that's likely to turn into a confrontation. Is the person bullheaded or flexible? The more you know, the more sensitively you can communicate your child's needs.

- *How do you recommend I register a complaint to make sure it's addressed and not ignored?* Even though you should respect the "chain of command," there are often "hidden" procedures or "secret" passages that can help you get what you need. A complaint that isn't logged— on paper or in the mind of someone with power—may not exist. Find out the best way to make sure yours is noticed.

- *If this happened to your child, how would you handle it?* Even though most parents want to know the answer to this question, they don't always ask it. Do so—realizing that it's an opinion and may not be the best approach for your situation and your child.

- *May I use your name as someone who's offered me advice, or do you prefer that I leave you out of it?* If you've received counsel from someone whose reputation is connected to those you find yourself at odds with, seek the person's permission before quoting him or her. He or she may be willing to offer advice, but only anonymously. It's understandable and acceptable for the person to refuse permission; respect his or her answer.

Twenty Questions

Once you've asked for initial clarification and help, the questions don't end. Here are some ideas to jump-start your additional fact-finding.

1. Ask for copies of records, tests, and evaluations that affect your child.

2. Ask the caregiver or service provider what areas of concern he or she sees.

Frame questions in a way that invites help, not defensiveness.

3. Ask whether the institution (school, clinic, league, etc.) has programs that help children with similar needs. Or will your child have to go to another site?

4. If this is a school matter, ask for a copy of your child's cumulative record (the file kept on him or her at the school). You may have to go to the district or county office and ask for this.

5. Ask the caregiver or service provider what chronic behaviors seem to get in the way of your child's success.

6. Ask specific questions. If your child is having difficulty completing homework, for instance, ask how it can be changed so that he can complete it.

7. Ask about options. Can your child record answers on tape? Can she get extra time to make it from one class to another? Can he sit at a table reserved for those with peanut allergies?

8. Ask whether there are other parents in the hospital, school district, or recreation program who have children with similar challenges; request their contact information (see #19).

9. When you ask about what accommodations can or should be made for your child, do so in a respectful tone.

10. Follow the chain of command when you make requests.

11. Frame questions in a way that invites help, not defensiveness. Ask, "What can we do to help Johnny stay focused in your class?" instead of, "Don't you think if you made your lessons more interesting Johnny would pay attention?"

12. During meetings, ask questions for clarification. Say, "Do you mean that you want me to check Jane's homework nightly, or that you want me to just sign off on it?"

13. Offer help, but ask first whether it will be accepted. Say, "I'm here to support you; is it acceptable to you if I check in with you weekly for a progress report?"

14. To avoid being rushed into making a bad decision, ask, "Is this solution time-sensitive, or am I permitted to take a while to think about it?"

15. Consult others for second opinions and wise counsel. Ask, "What has your experience been with this surgery?" or, "Is there another solution you know about that hasn't been offered to us?"

16. Exhaust other options before "going to war" for your child. In a school situation, for instance, go to the county or district office if your child's school can't seem to help. Ask, "Is there anything within the law that can help my child with this problem?"

17. If you think negotiations are on the brink of a breakdown, ask, "What can we do at this point to avoid invoking 'due process'?" Ask with sincerity and willing-

ness to try another avenue, so this question doesn't sound like a threat.

18. Find other parents who share your concern and ask them about their experiences. Don't stop there, though; develop proposals to solve a problem and present them to caregivers and service providers.

19. If an institution can't give you names of other parents, ask, "May I post my contact information on the office bulletin board?" It's kind of like being in college and looking for a roommate.

20. Ask other parents if they know about organizations that advocate for your child's particular needs—and join them.

The More You Know

To become effective advocates, we must be willing to look at our own strengths and weaknesses. Our strength lies in our relationship with our kids; our weaknesses can be defined by the information, expertise, and insights we don't have.

Overcoming our weaknesses requires a willingness to ask questions and track down answers. Information is power; to operate powerfully without stepping on toes, acquire as much information as you can.

8

PUTTING YOUR BEST FACE FORWARD

Guiding Principle #6:
*Consider carefully the self you want to
present to the world as a parent.*

I refuse to go out of the house without makeup. Without it, I look 12—and no one takes me seriously.

I've always looked younger than my years. Even though it's flattering at my age to be mistaken for someone younger, it hasn't always served me well.

The first year I taught, I was 22. I taught a high school learning disabilities class. Most of the students had been "left back" one or even two years, so many of them were only two years younger than I was!

Battling a strong intimidation factor from some of my students, I began to worry what their parents would think of me during our first parent-teacher conference. I didn't have to wait long to find out. Six weeks into the school year I hosted my first Open House night.

Mrs. Willard was the mom of one of my 19-year-old football players, Darren. He tormented me daily by asking for the bathroom pass and never returning to class. Already he was failing, and I knew I had to tell his mother.

"I know my son isn't the easiest student to teach," she said. "But you're his last chance."

Mrs. Willard intrigued me. I knew from her son's records that she worked in the food service industry and was a single parent. She had to take the bus to this conference. Wearing her "Sunday best," she sat with the polite demeanor of royalty—except when she nervously smoothed the hem of her dress.

"I'll admit that Darren is a challenge," I said, "but his needs still come first. Maybe we can come up with a plan together to get him to stay in class."

Suddenly Mrs. Willard morphed into a scarier version of herself. "Do you mean to tell me that boy is still skipping out on your class? I told him I'd whip his behind if he ever skipped again!"

Standing, she threw her pristine white gloves onto the floor. The proper "church lady" who'd walked submissively into my classroom had disappeared.

"I see that you're upset, Mrs. Willard," I said, trying to calm her. "We can work through this together."

It was as if she didn't hear me. "How can you let the boy walk all over you like that?" she demanded, towering over my desk. "You gotta give that boy some of your discipline!"

With my authority and ability to maintain classroom order questioned, my ego screamed for attention. *Who does she think she is? Maybe if she'd raised her boy better, there wouldn't be a problem.*

I couldn't say that, of course. But later, in the teacher's lounge, I registered my frustration about Mrs. Willard. I felt blindsided, lured into believing she was there to partner with me—only to find myself becoming a punching bag.

Many of the teachers had similar stories to tell. Their conferences had turned quickly and unexpectedly into confrontations, too.

Do You See What I See?

When your child's teachers retreat to the lounge, what do they say about you? When the coach commiserates with his assistants in the locker room, does your name come up? If so, how?

Our reputations often precede us into negotiations. What reputation do you want to project—and protect—when you support, defend, and champion your child?

Most of us choose the face we present to the world in order to get our children's needs met. Sometimes we conceal our flaws; at other times we highlight our best features. We try to put our best face forward to gain favor with "the other side."

To do this, we use a sort of makeup kit. And women aren't the only ones who do it. Here are the contents of that kit.

1. *Concealers.* Do you have circles under your eyes—the kind that reveal fatigue or allergies? Some of our weaknesses are obvious if we don't cover them up. When blemishes make us self-conscious, we don't operate at our best. If covering some of those up instills much-needed confidence, we should do it.

I'm not talking about deception. I'm talking about not distracting others from our message by putting our inadequacies on display.

For example, a tight writing deadline might be wearing me out. If I appear frazzled and preoccupied when I talk to a doctor, coach, teacher, or grandparent—and don't explain why—I risk being judged harshly and unfairly. My ability to advocate could be compromised.

Jessica, a young mother of two, found that self-doubt got in the way of her advocacy efforts. When she faced her family, trying to defend her choice to breast-feed her newborn, she didn't get far.

Her relatives disregarded her choice and even discouraged her. She was the first in her family to breast-feed, so the practice seemed unusual and ill-advised to parents who'd exclusively bottle-fed their babies.

When your child's teachers retreat to the lounge, what do they say about you?

It didn't help that Jessica was apprehensive and nervous. She wasn't sure she could nurse well or if her son would thrive. She belonged to a lactation support group, but hoped for the blessing of her family as well.

"It's my own fault," Jessica explains. "My inexperience and lack of self-assurance was front and center. I whined and complained to my mom and my sisters how difficult this was and how I felt like a failure. So they kept encouraging me to quit."

The face Jessica put forth was flecked with insecurity and her need for approval. That's all family members could see when they looked at her. Her "blemishes" distracted them from seeing what was most important to her.

"My lactation support group suggested that I not share with my family my frustration with breast-feeding, and leave that for our group to handle," she recalls. "I didn't want to be fake with my family, but then realized that I was just choosing what they saw—not trying to be someone I wasn't."

Concealing weaknesses can be productive during advocacy, but there's a line between covering up uncertainty and pretending to be someone you're not. The latter tends to erase the qualities that make you more human, more approachable—which can hinder negotiations.

Hiding flaws that distract also doesn't mean trying to make yourself look perfect. Believing that any appearance of weakness makes you vulnerable and ineffective can make you seem inflexible, unwilling to compromise.

This is especially true of men. "Society has tended to overvalue the idea of independence and self reliance in men to such an extent that any sign of weakness, any desire to ask for help, or any admission of vulnerability is seen as undesirable," writes Dr. Reamonn O'Donnchadha.[1]

Do you go too far in hiding your flaws? Or should you use a little cover-up to make a good impression on service providers who help care for your children? It's important to look in the mirror and check your makeup before someone else points it out to you in a less-than-flattering way.

2. *Highlighters.* I've been told that my eyes are my best feature. So I do what's been suggested to me by makeup artists—*play them up.* We all do this to some extent, accentuating certain areas we're confident about, as if to say, "Look at me! Pay attention!" The goal, however, should be to gain the right *kind* of attention.

We have to gain the interest of those with whom we negotiate before any real work can be done. Unless you call at least a little attention to yourself, your words will fall on deaf ears. You don't want to be so plain that you blend into the background like faded wallpaper. Yet screaming for attention like the gaudy gold around the necks of "new money" will only scare people away!

One of the best pieces of advice I've ever received was to "dress for the occasion." To feel comfortable in our skin and put others at ease, we need to dress, act, and favor our "best features" in ways that bring people together.

Walking into a meeting with a team of doctors to discuss treatment options for your daughter while wearing a micro-miniskirt, too much eye shadow, and chains rattling on your wrists may offer a pleasant distraction for certain professionals, but it erases any credibility you might have had. Knowing how to present yourself—whether it means using more inflection in your naturally expressive voice or displaying your knowledge of astronomy—can work to your child's advantage.

That happened to Yvette, who seemed to know more than the teacher did about what her daughter should learn in kindergarten.

"Julie didn't turn in a coloring page and her teacher went ballistic!" Yvette says. "She told me in the conference that all work must be turned in daily in their take-home folder. She made such a big deal over a coloring sheet."

As a teacher herself, Yvette understood the importance of students turning in their homework. But she also knew a few things about the lesser importance of coloring pages.

"I started to explain to her how much learning Julie did at home with me, but it didn't seem to matter," Yvette reports. "Julie knows everything about the llamas in Tibet, for Pete's sake. Not only was the coloring sheet a frivolous assignment, but it was completely unnecessary."

How did Yvette know that? Because she trained teachers in that district how to teach according to state standards—and coloring sheets were not part of the kindergarten requirements.

"She dropped her coloring sheet rampage after that," Yvette said. "I hated using the 'I know more than you know' card on her, but she didn't know who she was dealing with."

Yvette probably didn't endear herself to this teacher—but that wasn't her goal. By highlighting her experience and expertise, Yvette got the teacher to stop pressuring her daughter over coloring sheets. She didn't try to intimidate the teacher with her knowledge, but spoke with respect and clarity.

> Hiding flaws that distract doesn't mean trying to make yourself look perfect.

If you have an insight, skill, or experience whose mention can change the outcome of negotiation, call attention to it. In other words, if you've got it, flaunt it—without being obnoxious.

Problem Personalities

How would your child's principal, Sunday school teacher, or guidance counselor describe your personality? The Buddy and Bully tendencies described in Chapter 3 aren't the only possibilities. There are other "faces" that can complicate the process of standing up for your child.

Here are three parental personality profiles, grounded in the work of Carl Jung. These tendencies may make it more difficult to put your best face forward, hindering your progress at advocacy.

1. *The Joker.* Laura can't seem to get through a conversation without breaking out in giggles. She's not annoying or disruptive like a class clown, but apparently has a phobia about serious dialogue. She talks constantly, always carries a funny story up her sleeve, goes for the laugh, and is the life of the party. Believing silence is her enemy, threatening to reveal her insecurities, she fills up the space with jokes, puns, and sometimes tricks.

And her daughter's teacher doesn't know what to make of her.

Laura is charming, but that charm wears thin when teachers try to address her daughter's chronic absences that are beginning to get in the way of her learning. The daughter, who struggles with abnormally low blood pressure, sometimes faints at school. Laura knows how serious the situation is, but her "court jester" persona leads teachers to believe otherwise. Inside Laura agonizes over her daughter's absences, but doesn't know how to get help without appearing weak.

Ironically, what Laura perceives as weakness is valued by teachers as openness. If she doesn't stop clowning, she won't make the progress she so desires.

2. *Peter Pan.* "I don't want to grow up!" cried the leader of the Lost Boys of Neverland. This person is still in "child mode"—and usually attached to a mother or father figure during negotiations. Unable to make her own decisions, she submits too easily to the "authorities."

Take Sue, for instance. She's talking with her husband, Jon. Her best friend, Barbara, 10 years her senior, is seated nearby.

"I am so overwhelmed," Sue says. "I can't seem to get anything done. Having a baby sure changes everything."

"It's probably time to cut back on your outside work," Jon says. "I thought that was what we decided before she was born."

"I know, I know," Sue says. "But Barbara thinks it's better that I maintain my client load so I don't lose ground in my practice."

Irritated, Jon turns to look Barbara in the eye. "I don't mean any disrespect, Barbara, but this isn't about what *you* think. Sue and I need to do what's best for our child, and having Sue around more is best for our baby."

"That's fine," Barbara says. "But no one seems to be looking out for Sue's future, so it's up to me to do that."

Trying to head off an argument, Sue steps in. "Barbara's just trying to help," she tells Jon. "She's known me a long time."

"You mean she's known you longer than I have," Jon says, his patience wearing thin. Hearing the cries of their 10-month-old daughter, he heads for the back bedroom to tend to her. Sue and Barbara return to their conversation about building up Sue's business.

It's hard for Sue to stand up for her daughter if Barbara offers a conflicting point of view. Sue's childlike state makes her overly susceptible to suggestion from parental figures. Recognizing this tendency could be her first step toward becoming a more effective champion for her daughter.

3. *The Action Figure.* This parent is always on the go— addicted to work, sports, meetings, and friends. He or she never has time to take stock or hang out with the family. He or she is a "human doer" rather than a "human being."

The Action Figure focuses on the next task, never on enjoying the "now." If there's a problem with one of the children, he or she views it as a distraction to do away with. He or she will enter negotiations with an agenda and won't be swayed from the job at hand.

Female Action Figures are often described as "Marthas"—like the biblical friend of Jesus who tended to the urgent over the important and didn't know how to savor the moment (Luke 10:38-42). Martha's expectations are usually pretty high for the people in her life, including her children's teachers, doctors, coaches, and friends.

This is the parent who questions everything and who never seems satisfied with how things are progressing. This may sound like a good personality to have during advocacy, but the Action Figure doesn't catch the nuances of negotiation and often burns bridges. He or she needs to remember that there is joy not just in the destination, but in the journey.

Saving Face

When our youngest son was born, we battled one ear infection after another, beginning when he was two weeks old. Every time I took him to the pediatrician, I was asked the same set of questions:

"Does anyone in your household smoke?"

"No."

"Do you put him to sleep with a bottle?"

"No, I'm breast-feeding."

"Is he in daycare?"

"No."

Every month we got a new antibiotic prescription. Every month we got less sleep. Every month he ate less.

I was getting really concerned. The phrase "failure to thrive" haunted me. My self-image as a new mom was threatened. The doctor's expert status intimidated me to the point that I didn't question his diagnosis.

By six months my son had his first set of drainage tubes put in his ears. By about seven months feeding him became a battle. When it was time, he would put his little hands out in protest and cry. I felt rejected and helpless.

By eight months he still wasn't babbling. He couldn't sit up without eventually toppling over.

Then friends from one of my support groups suggested something that blew my mind: "He's probably allergic to milk."

I immediately took this nugget of information to our pediatrician, hoping he'd be as excited about this discovery as I was. But he immediately dismissed it.

"But you don't know what's causing his chronic nasal congestion and resulting ear infections," I said. "I think this is worth investigating."

"I doubt a milk allergy is the case," he said with unreasonable authority.

He stood his ground. It was clear that he wasn't willing to risk "losing face" for my sake.

The next day I put myself on a no-dairy diet and took a calcium supplement. I figured that since my milk was my son's only food source, what I ate had to matter. It was a hard change to make—but within days my baby stopped putting up a fuss at feeding time.

Within weeks he was eating more than he ever had; a month later he'd reached a normal weight. The nasal congestion and ear infections were gone.

I was right. Our pediatrician was wrong and unwilling to admit it.

I changed pediatricians.

Conflict often throws us into "face-saving" mode. We may put our interests ahead of the other side's—even ahead of our children's. No one wants to look bad, so we do what it takes to protect our images in front of others. When both parties make face-saving the top priority, a standoff can occur and no progress will be made.

The priority should be to build relationships with your child's caregivers and service providers, not to save face. This usually means putting the other parties' needs on a plane with your own. As Philippians 2:4 puts it, "Do not merely look out for your own personal interests, but also for the interests of others."

In my confrontation with the pediatrician, he wasn't the only one who wanted to save face. My image as a mom was threatened, too. Unfortunately, when saving face is more important than resolving conflict, this usually results in a parting of ways.

Being Open-Faced

Does putting your best face forward mean covering the real one with a mask? Not at all. In fact, being at least somewhat "open-faced" usually helps your cause when you're standing up for your child.

If you tend to encase your face when negotiating, here are five alternatives to consider.

1. *Let at least some of your feelings show.*

Have you ever talked with someone you couldn't "read"? His facial expressions remained emotionless; even if you provoked him, he remained cool and calm and almost robot-like. How did this make you feel? Did it put you at ease, or did you wonder what the person was really thinking?

There's a delicate balance between keeping your feelings in

check and appearing emotionless. When you're dealing with issues surrounding your child, you want to know the person on the other side of the table cares. Relationships aren't nurtured without emotion; if you hope to build a relationship with this service provider or caregiver for your child's sake, it's important that you let each other see some of what's going on under the surface.

When both parties make face-saving the top priority, a standoff can occur and no progress will be made.

You can't force the other person to be transparent, of course. But you can decide to be transparent yourself. Don't reveal so much that your emotions become distracting; you want to be transparent, not make your opponent wish you were invisible.

2. Reveal your decision-making process.

When you don't reveal how you reached a conclusion, you confuse those on the other side of the conversation. Confusion can lead to mistrust, which does nothing to accomplish the goals of advocacy.

Consider this scenario, in which a teacher was the offender.

"I checked your grades online today," Sandy told her 14-year-old son. "You want to explain how you managed to get a D on an extra-credit paper?"

"What?" Justin asked. "I thought that was just for extra points, not a grade."

"That's what *I* thought," Sandy said. "Don't worry. I already e-mailed your teacher to ask about it. This really pulls your grade down."

The next day the teacher replied to Sandy's e-mail. The message went something like this:

I'm always happy to hear from parents who stay involved in
their children's education, and by checking on their grades
online, you've shown me you are one of those parents.
After the students turned in their extra-credit assignment I
decided that I would use it for a real grade instead. I realized
that we just didn't have enough grades for this quarter, so
since they all already did the assignment I decided to count
it. Sorry for the confusion.

That was it—no further explanation or acknowledgment
that this decision could change Justin's overall grade. Sandy was
furious, and her e-mailed response showed it: "How could you
change your mind like that after the fact and not tell parents, let
alone the students? Justin would have put more thought into
the assignment if he'd known ahead of time that it would count
against him if he didn't."

The teacher's reply: "I'm sorry this caused any confusion.
Hopefully Justin will do better next quarter."

Two weeks later, right before report cards came out, the
assignment was dropped from online grades. The teacher had
changed her mind yet again, without saying a word. Though
this decision worked in Justin's favor, it created an atmosphere
of distrust surrounding teacher, students, and parents.

You can't make your opponent reveal her decision-making
process, but you can be candid about your own. Let others see
how you got from point A to point B.

3. *Put your cards on the table.*

When you do this, you're usually saying, "Look, I realize
this may seem like a lost cause to you, but I'm going to lay it all
on the line so you can see what's at stake here."

Does this make you vulnerable? Definitely. Does it make you appear weak? Possibly. But it's not the same as offering your throat to a wolf; it's more like humbly stating your case and throwing yourself on the mercy of the court.

It's important that those with whom you negotiate know what's at stake. Compassion often follows this revelation, but there are no guarantees.

4. *Offer a behind-the-scenes tour.*

When I was in high school, our choir got a backstage look at Walt Disney World. We were led through hidden doors off Main Street to an underground we never knew existed—half-costumed characters on break, automatons being refurbished, golf carts full of performers being transported to their stages on street level. I gained a greater appreciation for that "magical" kingdom, knowing what it takes to put on such a production.

Letting people in on why you're fighting so hard for your child can do the same thing. Does the person at the other side of the table know this is the third year that your son has struggled in math, and only math? Does your daughter's ballet teacher know her class is the only thing that gets your daughter through the week, so encouraging her to quit just isn't going to happen?

Being "open-faced" in this way helps the "other side" understand—and maybe appreciate—why you're working so hard to stand up for your child.

5. *Let them see you sweat.*

This recommendation may make you a little uncomfortable; feel free to reject it.

Sometimes the best way to gain friends and influence people is to present them with the unexpected. How would you react if a supposedly hard-nosed father looked into your eyes and said,

"She's my baby girl. She's worked so hard to come this far. Just give her 10 minutes to show you why she deserves this audition"?

You'd probably be caught off guard, your curiosity piqued. You'd want to see what had made this usually stone-faced man melt.

My mother said not to wear my heart on my sleeve; I'd only get hurt. I learned that I got hurt regardless. So now when I go to battle on behalf of our children, I try to let out the passion that guides me—not in a destructive way, but in a way that honors my love for my children and for God.

This approach may not be for everyone. But if you can manage it, give them a glimpse of your heart.

Four More Face Facts

Putting your best face forward isn't just a matter of "looking good." It helps define how you stand up for your child, and whether your efforts are effective. Here are four more principles to remember about how to come across as an advocate.

1. *Sometimes you need to "fix your face."*

You can do this for yourself, backpedaling from a statement when you realize it's led your opponent to see you in a negative light. You can do it for someone else, taking the blame for your spouse's tardiness at a meeting you scheduled. We fix our faces in a variety of ways when we detect that someone doesn't see "our side" as we want to be seen.

I admit that in the ear infection episode, I didn't spend much time trying to fix my face for that pediatrician. I wasn't interested in resolving the conflict at that point; I just wanted to move on. When conflicts like these arise, you can either fix your face so that you're perceived as a "friend" again, or accept the fact that you no longer look the same to the other person—and that this conflict probably will not be resolved. You always have a choice.

In another case, fixing my face was important to me. When one of my sisters expressed frustration with the fact that her son wasn't challenged in school, my ears perked up. I could help; I taught gifted students, and had written a book for parents on gifted children. This was right up my alley. But each time I tried to offer advice, it was swatted away like a bothersome fly. My sister didn't see me as anyone but her sister.

So I fixed my face, wanting her to see me as the expert she sought. I asked her whether the teacher had initiated a referral to have her son tested for the gifted program. I asked whether a conference had been scheduled to discuss his needs. I outlined the gifted characteristics I recognized in my nephew, her son.

By asking questions that only someone "on the inside" would ask, and by assuring her that I knew her son well, I finally appeared to her as more than just a sister. She could see me for who I really was—the helper she needed.

2. *Sometimes you need to "show your face."*

When you show your face, you're saying, "He's with me." This does more than get you into an exclusive nightclub or backstage at a concert; it's a compassionate move on your part. It's another opportunity to follow the example of Jesus, who shows His face on our behalf when He acts as our gateway to heaven.

Standing up for your child is a way of showing your face on your child's behalf. You can also show your face for the benefit of a spouse or friend who's on your side in the advocacy process.

This isn't always easy. Dorothy, a divorced mom, found it hard to show her face for the sake of her ex-husband. Theirs had been a difficult marriage and an even more difficult divorce; the four children they shared had suffered greatly.

As the custodial parent, Dorothy stayed in close contact with her children's teachers. Her ex-husband, Rob, didn't. Though he received the same conference notices, report cards, and invitations that she did, Dorothy was often the only one to show up. Rob always had an excuse. Dorothy was tired of showing her face to make his look more acceptable.

When you choose to spend a bit of your credibility for the sake of someone else, it's best to do it without regard to how it makes you look. Are you afraid you'll resemble a doormat? Remember how Jesus stands up for us. Look for ways to build up your allies and even opponents as well as your child.

3. *Sometimes you need to "get in their face"—but carefully.*

What's the difference between being assertive and being aggressive? Can you get in someone's face and still put your best face forward?

Carol explains her approach this way: "I never go in trying to step on anyone, but if someone doesn't hear what I am saying or tries to pretend it isn't really a problem, I will certainly speak my mind. I have upset and hurt some teachers' feelings, but I am highly respected in my children's Christian high school, and my calls and e-mails are always immediately returned."

The truth is that you can't really know what other people think of you. If they don't say, "I highly respect you," don't assume they do.

To ensure that your child's needs are addressed during a conflict or negotiation, you need to express yourself clearly, persist with your goals in the face of opposition, and *appropriately* stand up for yourself and your child. Your goal should be to come to workable compromise and agreement. You're looking for a win-win outcome.

Here are three ways to stay appropriate while getting in someone's face:

- Be self-disclosing. Reveal aspects of your history (or your child's), opinions, values, and aspirations. This helps to put your opponents at ease and enhance the relationship.

- Be persistent. When battling a bureaucracy or facing consistent resistance, you may have to sound like a broken record by saying over and over what you want—without anger, irritation, or yelling.

- Cope with criticism. This may mean agreeing with it, at least in principle—saying, "Yes, I should have returned the permission slip to you on time." It may mean offering negative information about yourself, saying, "I'm definitely deadline-challenged." It may mean getting to the heart of the problem, saying, "Do you have any additional criticisms you'd like to share?" But it doesn't mean getting defensive.

4. *If you must "face off," do it fairly.*

When we feel threatened, the "fight or flight" instinct kicks in. We choose either to face the threat or avoid it. If you choose to stay and make a stand, remember to do it fairly. Here are some ways to do that:

- Don't ambush. Make an appointment; don't just show up unannounced.

- Present your argument logically. Keep emotion out of it.

- Listen carefully to the other party. Restate the "other side's" point in your own words to make sure you understand it.
- Stick to the issue. It's easy to get sidetracked. Stay in the present.
- Agree on what behavior is acceptable. This can be as simple as, "Let's both take a seat," or "Let's try to keep a civil tongue."
- Keep all blows above the belt. Don't "push buttons" or attack sensitive areas if known to you.
- If you can't settle the issue, table it for now. Call a temporary truce if you're not getting anywhere; reschedule to allow time for rethinking, recovering, and reconsidering.
- If you can agree, decide on a plan of action—who'll do what and by when.
- If you're later dissatisfied with the outcome, make an appointment for another discussion. Silence means agreement; if the proposed solution didn't work out, go back to the table and say so.[2]

Who Do You See When You Look at Me?

Faith-based parenting answers to a higher calling than our egos and self-images. Concerns about our "faces" are about more than looking good.

If we pretend to be something we're not in order to gain favor for ourselves and our children, we're not putting our best face forward. God knows our heart, and in the end this choice can undermine our efforts to get what we "deserve."

We all need to remember that everything we gain is by God's

grace alone. Every good thing comes from Him. Even the things for which you negotiate on your child's behalf ultimately come as a result of God's amazing grace.

If you have a relationship with God, your advocacy efforts point to Him. When caregivers and service providers look at us, they should see His face reflected in ours.

They may not always like what they see. But try to make sure they see Him first and you second when you work on behalf of your children.

9

LEARNING TO STAND ASIDE

Guiding Principle #7:
Let your children see how it's done;
then step back and let them do it.

I sat in the school auditorium with trepidation. I'd rehearsed this speech over and over, trying to figure out the best approach.

Our oldest son, Christopher, was ready to start middle school—but not in the traditional way. I had a lot to prove if the school was going to accept him.

We'd homeschooled our children through elementary school. Christopher had expressed a strong desire to return to public school if the right program came along—and it had. The International Baccalaureate program at our local middle school promised to challenge him.

It was important for Christopher to communicate to the principal what he'd learned and why he believed he'd succeed in this program. But we didn't have report cards to show in order to prove he was qualified for this program. I had only the portfolio I'd kept on his progress; we had bound it like a book and included photos and a multimedia presentation on a disk.

Now it was time for our conference with the principal.

"We're looking for students willing to work hard," he said. "We look for quality workers, and I need to see from you and your son that he is that kind of student."

"I may not have traditional grades to show you, Mr. Batin," I said. "But I do have samples of Christopher's work that I think fit what you're looking for."

Page by page, Christopher and I went through the portfolio with the principal. I explained what I intended my son to learn from each assignment, and Christopher explained what he learned.

An independent study project caught the principal's eye. "Tell me about this," he said. "This looks like a pretty complex project."

Christopher's eyes lit up. "Mom and Dad were going to Italy for a week, so we decided to study Italy in preparation," he began. "We started with its history and mythology and how the language developed. We made a topographic salt map and even recreated a Roman bath in our bathtub and then swimming pool."

Mr. Batin was fascinated. Christopher went on to show him the 100 Latin word roots he learned and how this led to his new interest in Greek word roots and Greek mythology.

"I thought maybe I'd compare and contrast the Greek and Roman mythologies," he explained. "They have most of the same gods, just with different names."

"Is this all you have to show me?" Mr. Batin asked.

"I do have his state test scores," I said, pulling out the report. "Christopher took the test even though he's not required to, and we did it at our own expense."

"This is a good showing," Mr. Batin said. "We'll seriously consider Christopher's application to our program."

Afraid that we still hadn't convinced him, I laid all my cards on the table.

"Mr. Batin, I realize you have only so many slots available in this program, and we appreciate the time you've taken with us tonight," I began. "I'm happy to continue homeschooling my son if this doesn't work out. I just want you to know that we did our homework and believe this is the right fit for our son. I don't easily give that kind of trust, but I want you to know that we're willing to take a chance if you are."

"I appreciate that," he said. "Thank you for your honesty."

Six weeks later we received an acceptance letter. I was glad I hadn't held back during our meeting—and that Christopher hadn't, either. Like Christopher, most children learn how to stand up for themselves by watching us do it for them. In this chapter we'll explore that process.

Helping Kids Stand on Their Own

"When my daughter was in the fourth grade, her anxiety and distaste for school got worse and worse," Linda explains. "She always had a ready excuse for not wanting to go to school. She feigned stomachaches and other general aches and pains, and it worked on me for awhile. When I stopped letting her stay home, she found a sympathetic ear in the school counselor, who let her avoid class."

Linda realized that her daughter Kelly's chronic health complaints were symptomatic of a deeper problem. Yes, she hated school, but doesn't everyone? Kelly complained almost for the sake of complaining, and it didn't solve anything.

"I'm bored," Kelly told Linda. "The teacher treats the boys better than the girls— and when she explains math, she goes on and on, talking way too much."

Linda finally suggested they schedule a conference with the teacher.

"Since I wasn't in the classroom with firsthand knowledge, Kelly needed to be the one to lead the conference," Linda says. "Kelly was scared at the thought of confronting her teacher, but I assured her that I would sit right next to her during the meeting."

At this school, standard procedure at conferences was for teachers to review a list of strengths, weaknesses, and goals for students. Linda suggested that Kelly consider using this format in the meeting; maybe her concerns would be better received.

"I was very proud of Kelly for the courage and maturity she displayed in approaching her teacher," Linda says. "Though it didn't solve all of Kelly's issues in the classroom, she learned many lifelong lessons from this experience, such as how to approach a problem and cooperatively work towards a resolution."

Children can and should stand up for themselves, but often aren't equipped to do so. Good coaches know the power of showing their prodigies how it's done—and then supporting their efforts to attain their goals.

Four Strengths for Standing Up

Letting go and letting kids "go it alone" is one of the hardest things a parent must do. Since the 1960s, parents have gotten more and more involved in their children's lives, for better and for worse.

For the sake of our children, we must give them what they need to live life on their own. Our job is to help them soar, not to ground them or handicap their efforts at independence by clipping their wings.

Helping kids leave the nest begins with helping them to develop four crucial character traits. As you read through the following section, try to mentally measure your child's progress in these areas.

Our job is to help kids soar, not to ground them or handicap their efforts at independence by clipping their wings.

1. *Initiative.* This is the ability to act on your own. Many parents pray their children will acquire this trait, but inadvertently keep that from happening by intervening too often. Kids take the initiative when they feel capable; if they don't feel capable, they hesitate.

Angie, a divorced mother of four children and two stepchildren, explains her initial failing in this area: "I'm working very hard at some tough love. Saying 'no' is really hard. It puts uncomfortable pressure on my kids that I'd rather fix. But I am not doing them any favors fixing everything so that they never learn themselves. All I've taught them with my rescue behavior is that I am at their beck and call."

Angie's children never took the initiative to solve their own problems. They waited on Mom to "fix things" so they could go on with their lives. Their father's relationship with his children was immature and unreliable; Angie tried to protect them from the resulting disappointment, but it backfired on her. Her children came to see her as a doormat instead.

"Right now I'm respecting myself," she says. "By modeling my worth, I am teaching my children that they have worth. When I modeled 'I'll solve everything,' I taught them that they were not capable.

"I've had to teach my children how to cook, shop, and take care of themselves. Now I know they can handle it when they are away (at their dad's). They will not go hungry or have an empty refrigerator at their dad's anymore. I wish I had learned this earlier. Let go and let God care for me and my children."

Initiative isn't caught like a cold—it's taught. If you want your children to take the first step to attain a goal or solve a problem, you must teach them how—and then step back and watch.

2. *Responsibility.* To be responsible is to be accountable. Responsibility begins at home, but spreads into the wide world as children grow into adulthood. You can foster responsibility in your children by teaching them how to care for someone or something—a pet, for example—and backing off to let them do it on their own.

Household chores offer plenty of opportunities to hone this trait. Kids need plenty of practice to perfect a skill, so don't rush in to finish the job for them if they don't do it just right the first time. Let them practice in a safe environment.

Here are two tips for making the most of these opportunities:

- Choose chores that are developmentally appropriate. It's not a matter of age, it's a matter of ability. Just because your seven-year-old *should* be able to make his bed, it doesn't mean that he *can*. The fact that you didn't mow the lawn until you were fourteen doesn't mean your twelve-year-old isn't able. Assign chores based on what's needed *and* what your child can do well. Success breeds success; to foster responsibility, set your kids up to succeed.

- Show them how it's done. Ever expected your child to clean his room on Saturday morning but discovered on Saturday night that the job never got finished? Maybe he (a) has a different understanding of "clean" than you do, or (b) doesn't know how to do the job well. Take a few moments to show him exactly how you expect a chore to be done; then supervise him as he does it himself. Eventually he'll be able to complete the task without your supervision.

3. *Self-confidence.* When you have self-confidence, you believe in your ability to succeed. Lacking this trait can inhibit your ability to stand up for yourself.

"Every aptitude test I ever took spit out a long list of things I'd be good at," Cal says. "The jobs those tests suggested might be a good fit for me sounded interesting, but I couldn't get excited over any of them. Basically I had no idea what I wanted to do."

Cal needed more than an aptitude test to give him the confidence to pursue a goal. He needed his parents to encourage him to pursue his interests, even if they didn't show up on those test results.

"All I knew was that I loved cars," Cal continues. "But to me all that pointed to was to become a mechanic. I lived in a house with parents who expected all their children to go to college and even pursue postgraduate degrees. Automotive careers didn't quite fit that vision."

Unfortunately, Cal never pursued his dreams. In fact, he forgot how to dream.

"I didn't have enough confidence to go after what I wanted, in spite of what everyone else said I should do," he said. "It wasn't really a matter of pleasing them; it was more a matter of not knowing my own mind or my own heart. Even now I don't know how to pursue goals. I wouldn't even know where to start."

Let your kids see how you approach advocacy, so that they know how it's done.

Children gather confidence little by little as a rolling snowball collects snow. You can build your child's confidence by encouraging him to investigate, pursue, and practice things in which he's interested and gifted. Encourage him to take risks, to try new things—instead of doing everything for him.

4. *Diligence.* To stand up for themselves effectively, kids must persevere. Diligence is one of the most challenging traits to instill in our children; think of all the times you've complained about a job left unfinished or follow-up left incomplete. Your job is to encourage and expect your kids to follow through on tasks they'd prefer not to do at all.

When my mother died and I went through her closet, it was filled with unfinished projects—needlepoint, crochet, craft kits of all kinds. The urgent usually overtakes the important, but diligence helps us achieve the latter.

Children are often more easily distracted than adults. Try minimizing distractions to help your kids persist in what's important. Whether it's finishing homework, practicing piano, mowing the lawn, applying for college scholarships, watching the neighbor's pets when they're out of town, or standing up for themselves, diligence is what gets the job done.

Know Your Position

Good coaches will tell you that one of the most important things for a player is to know his position. As you coach your child about self-advocacy, there are two positions to know—yours and his.

You are the coach, not the player. Your child is the player, and needs to embrace that position with the confidence that comes from practice.

Good coaches can demonstrate the skills they want to instill in their players. It's hard to take a baseball coach seriously if he can't hit the ball himself. Let your kids see how you approach advocacy, so that they know how it's done.

"I was driving toward the school to pick up my stepdaughter when I saw this group of kids start to beat up on another boy on the side of the road," Carrie remembers. "Recently, I'd watched a news special report about how the public responds to acts of violence with kids they don't know, so it was fresh in my mind.

"I immediately pulled over and began to yell at the kids to stop. I said, 'Do I need to call the police?' They just looked at me silent and dumbfounded. I repeated, 'Do I need to call the police? I expect an answer from you right now.'

"Finally, they said they understood. Then I told them, 'You cannot hit other kids!' I was amazed at my reaction to defend a child I didn't even know. My adrenaline was flowing and I was shaking by the time my stepdaughter got into the car. When I told her what happened, she couldn't believe I'd do that for a stranger. I truly believe she gained assurance from the fact that I could stand up for a kid I didn't know."

It's one thing to tell kids to stand up for themselves or someone else; it's another to let them see you in action. The question isn't whether you *are* a coach; it's whether you'll be intentional in your coaching.

Practice, Practice, Practice

Learning a new skill isn't something you can pick up on the first try. Fortunately, there are chances for kids to practice the skills of self-advocacy every day.

Think of all the things you do *for* your children. How many could they do for themselves? Give kids as many chances as possible to practice these skills until they become a natural part of who they are—a phenomenon coaches call "muscle memory."

If your son wants to know how much a particular video game costs at his favorite store, do you call the store for him? Or do you point him to the Yellow Pages to find the number and make the call himself?

If your daughter had a fight with her best friend and wants to reconcile, do you call the other girl's parents to arrange the meeting? Or do you encourage your daughter to make the call herself?

If your 12-year-old son walks in after a game of touch football declaring his hunger, do you rush to make him a snack? Or do you lovingly remind him where the refrigerator is?

Help can quickly turn into "enabling," which in turn disables your children. Keep your eyes and ears open for ways to get them to practice getting their needs met on their own—with your supervision.

The time to start is now. The older children get, the higher the stakes become. Missing the deadline to audition for the school play is disappointing; missing the deadline to apply for college financial aid can be disastrous. Forgetting your homework jeopardizes your grades; forgetting a project at your company jeopardizes your livelihood. Saying nothing while a classmate bullies your friend on the playground is shameful; saying nothing while your spouse is harassed can be dangerous.

While the stakes are still relatively low, train children how to stand firm, stand tall, and stand up for themselves.

Make It Safe

Facing a stand-up-for-yourself situation can be frightening, even paralyzing. You can walk your child through these challenges ahead of time by role-playing—presenting hypothetical situations and offering "game plans" to rehearse.

Lane role-plays with her children. "If someone asks them to smoke, sneak out, take a drink, etc., I help them with answers so that if they get in that situation they will be prepared."

When our son Christopher was in kindergarten, his teacher did a good job of preparing her students for the probability of bullying on the playground. She encouraged parents to act out her suggestions with our children so that they'd be able to stand up for themselves. "I can't be everywhere to protect them," she said. Parents can voice the same sentiment.

"What do you do if another boy or girl is bothering you or pushing you or trying to hurt you?" I asked Christopher.

"I look at him and say, 'Stop (whatever the bully is doing).'"

"What if he doesn't listen and does it again?"

"I look at him again and tell him again to stop."

"What if he still doesn't listen?" I asked.

"Then I find the nearest grown-up and tell them that he's bothering me and that I told him two times to stop."

It was hard to tell whether Christopher was ready for such a confrontation. But we didn't have long to wait to find out. A week later he came home more puzzled than upset.

"During gym class a boy I don't know ran after me and started calling me names," he said.

"And what did you do?" I kept my fingers crossed as I waited for his answer.

"I stopped running, looked at him, and told him to stop chasing me. I told him two times, Mom," he said.

"Did he stop?"

"No. He did it again. He wouldn't stop." Christopher was visibly upset now.

"Did you find the nearest grown-up to tell them?"

"I forgot to do that part."

"How about we try something a little different?" I suggested. "If he does it again, tell him to stop just like before. But if he doesn't, do something that will surprise him."

"Like what?" Christopher said, intrigued.

"Ask him what his name is and if he'd like to play with you. Then, if that doesn't work, go find a grown-up. Some kids pick on other kids because they have no friends. Maybe no one has ever asked him to play before."

That made sense to our son's five-year-old brain. The next day he tried the plan.

"I told him to stop and he wouldn't," he reported after school. "Then I just looked at him and said, 'My name is Chris. What's your name?' His name is Jack, Mom. He didn't want to play with me, but he stopped chasing me. I didn't have to go find a grown-up nearby."

I didn't know if this solution would last. But I did know that our son now felt in control of a situation that could have made him feel powerless.

There are thousands of situations that may require your children to stand up for themselves. This book can't address them all, but teaching your kids the basics of self-advocacy will give them the tools to meet most future challenges.

At the very least, make sure your children know the following:

- when and how to make a 911 emergency call
- how to seek help from a teacher when they don't understand an assignment
- how to speak up to you or someone else if they have a concern about health or abuse
- how to budget their time to complete a project
- how to get information they need to succeed from coaches and other mentors
- how to let their friends' parents know what they are and aren't allowed to do while away from home
- how to get home if their ride falls through

There are many more situations you can and should prepare your child for; try getting your family together for a brainstorming session and make a list that applies to your household.

Steps to Standing Up

When you teach a new concept—like self-advocacy—and want it to stick, experts recommend the following four steps.

1. *Model it.* When you model something, you're really putting on a show. Maybe it's not as dramatic as a full theatrical production, but it's a show nevertheless. Children learn more from this show than they do from what you tell them.

This first step is crucial. Take time to carefully demonstrate to your child how to handle a particular situation. Go step by step; don't rush.

Michelle knows firsthand the power of the show.

"Jeremy was recently harassed by some bullies at school and on the bus," she explains. "I called the school, met with the principal, etc., with no success. I finally realized that Jeremy needed to learn to fend for himself (at least a little bit) and that he probably didn't know how."

It's easy to assume kids know how to do "basic" things, but you may be surprised to discover how clueless they often are. Use this as an opportunity to show your child what to do.

"I told him that every time they approached him to say anything or threaten him, that he should point his index finger straight at them and in his loudest voice, without hollering, say, 'Leave me alone!' I told him to say it over and over again until they walked away and to do it every time they tried to say something to him. Praise the Lord! Within a week, those boys left him alone and haven't tried bothering him since. Giving him the words gave him power. It was such a thrill for both of us!"

2. *Guided practice—do it with them.* Explain to your kids again how it works, and then do it *with* them. This creates a safety net as they practice their new skill. You're right there to jump in if needed, and it sets them up to succeed.

At this point you're still guiding them through the process, reminding them of critical steps. You're still free to interrupt the process, if necessary, and show them again how to do it, before returning to the task at hand.

Sandy helped her daughter stand up to boys who mistreated her at school. Her daughter felt powerless and didn't know how to respond to their behavior. Sandy hadn't had a chance to model a response; she had to jump right into guided practice.

"One young man wrote something very inappropriate in her yearbook and left his cell phone number," Sandy says. "I instinctively called the young man and asked him to have no contact with her and [said] he would be in serious trouble if I knew of further harassment."

Sandy did model for her daughter how to handle this boy. She did it with her daughter standing right there.

"While I know it embarrassed her, I also know she felt secure knowing I stood up for her," Sandy adds. "She is learning to stand up for herself, and she knows that when she faces hard issues that we are there to support her."

Confronting another boy on the phone with the same issue would become easier for Sandy's daughter. Sandy would stand right there and give her the words if she faltered; if need be, she'd interrupt the call to say the right thing if her daughter needed her to.

"My belief is that God has placed me in her life, and one day I will stand before God," Sandy says. "I am responsible for my response to what happens in her life. What others think is not my primary motivation."

Since then, Sandy's daughter has come home with stories about standing up to people who were spreading rumors about her. "I believe the most important lesson has been that as a child of God she is worth standing up for," Sandy concludes. "People will try to cross her boundaries. That's human nature, and she does not have to allow it to happen. She can say 'no' and speak out against lies."

3. *Supervised practice—watch them do it.* At this point you're still giving reminders on how it's done: "Remember to introduce yourself. Remember to thank them for their time. Remember to look them in the eye when you speak."

Provide those reminders before your child walks into the situation. Then step back and watch.

Be there when he's on the phone asking his boss for time off. Be there when she leads a conference with her teacher. Be there when he confronts his coach about unfair treatment. But be a silent witness at this point.

> As much as you want to continue being the hero in your child's life, you must step aside if he's to stand up for himself.

Dana's daughter chose to attend boarding school in her sophomore year, due to intense family struggles at home. It wasn't the ideal situation for supervising a child's attempts at self-advocacy, but Dana made it work.

"I drove down to Jenna's school to stay for a period of time every month," she explains. "I made sure I was in contact with administrators and even the campus nurses. Everyone at that school who was involved in any way with my daughter knew my name even though I lived hundreds of miles away.

"Several times I had to step in when I felt a fellow student or teacher had really crossed the line of appropriate behavior, but on many occasions Jenna would handle issues herself and let me know afterwards what had transpired."

Debriefing after an incident is helpful during this stage. Let your child tell you how he handled the situation; ask questions for clarification if necessary. Offer suggestions only if your child isn't satisfied with the outcome or seeks your advice. Keep armchair-quarterback judgments to yourself; otherwise, you risk making your child feel he isn't capable of doing this on his own.

"As a result Jenna grew in her faith and in her leadership abilities," Dana reports. "By the end of the year, the girls' volleyball coach and football coach were discussing faith issues in their office and incorporating biblical principles on the field and the volleyball court. How cool is that?" Even from a distance Dana could revel in her daughter's success at standing up for herself.

4. *Independent practice—let them do it themselves.* This is the hardest step! Give your child the directions once again, then walk away.

You've given her all she needs to stand up for herself. It's time for you to step aside. Her success or failure is up to her and reflects only on her; it has nothing to do with you now.

Your child will learn from successes and failures—probably more from failures. If you try to protect her from failing by stepping in when it's not your turn, you short-circuit her progress.

Overinvolved parents can disable capable kids. The truth is that children will make mistakes, fail, and won't always get what they need or want. No matter how well you prepare them, this life will not be trouble free.

You can model for your child what God modeled for us when He sent His Son. As much as the disciples didn't want Jesus to leave them, He had to. As much as you want to continue being the hero in your child's life, you must step aside if he's to stand up for himself.

Lord, Let Me Decrease

Our influence as parents is temporary. There comes a time when that influence must decrease.

Remember when your toddler proclaimed, "I do it!" when you tried to do things for him? His instincts were right. Our instincts to coddle and protect can delay our children's necessary maturity.

John the Baptist said it best when he told his followers, "He must increase, but I must decrease" (John 3:30). His life and ministry pointed his followers to the Messiah. John paved the way for Jesus' coming, but then humbly stepped aside.

Can you do that for your children when the time comes? The prospect of the empty nest can be one of joy, not sorrow. You'll have regrets—words left unsaid and words you'll wish you could take back—but if you've prepared your kids to stand up for themselves, you can celebrate.

WHEN YOUR BEST ISN'T GOOD ENOUGH

Guiding Principle #8:
Trust in the certainty of your calling.

"I wasn't a Christian when I first became pregnant," Diane said. "In fact, I was unmarried and homeless. I guess you could say I was a prodigal. I hadn't been in contact with my own family for a number of years."

She adjusted the collar on her Goodwill blouse and took a deep breath. Explaining to others why she no longer had custody of her two children was always difficult. It made her feel so weak, and often humiliated.

"It wasn't until my daughter was born that I even attempted to contact my own mother," Diane continued. "After two abortions and now having a child out of wedlock, it wasn't easy for me to show up after all those years and say, 'Hey, Mom, you're a grandmother!'"

She paused to regain her composure. Finally she continued, "It's funny. I thought she'd just slam the door in my face when I showed up after letting her think I was dead for five years. But she didn't. She welcomed me back into her embrace and her life, and she accepted my little girl without question."

Diane's story doesn't end there, nor does it have a fairy-tale ending. She had another child, this time a son, with the same man who fathered her first child. They lived together for several years.

Diane returned to alcohol abuse. She had difficulty holding a job. Her children suffered the effects of her addictions, and had a wide variety of learning and behavioral problems once they entered school.

Finally she and her partner separated. He took the children to live with him and his mother. Diane relinquished her parental rights.

How can she ever stand up for her children now?

When We Miss the Mark

You may be tempted to read Diane's story and judge her past, saying, "This is a direct consequence of her sin." You'd be right, but that's not what this chapter is about. It's about how to stand up for your child when things don't go the way they're supposed to.

Sometimes, despite your best efforts, you can't advocate effectively for your child. We all fall short of perfect parenting, and there are times when our best just isn't good enough.

There's the single working mother whose children spend more time in before- and after-school programs than they do with her. There's the father who's incarcerated and unable to do anything to stand up for his children on the outside.

When things go wrong, it's not always because you've failed.

Perhaps your child has broken the law, and you watch helplessly as the court-appointed lawyer becomes his advocate. Or maybe you're a grandmother who finds herself having to raise a grandchild—without the resources you had 20 years ago. What does advocacy mean for you?

Whatever the causes of your challenges, you're the one God chose to care for this child. I've said it before and I'll say it again: If you believe in His sovereignty, you must believe that you're not a caregiver by accident—even if you didn't plan it that way. When things go wrong, it's time to regroup and find another way to be an advocate.

If you find yourself in a less-than-ideal parenting situation, take a step back and see what arrows you still have in your hands. Even one arrow, when carefully aimed, can hit the mark!

Laying Your Isaac Down

At 12:35 A.M. Gene blindly reached for the bedside phone. Bleary-eyed and foggy, he had to work hard to focus on what was being said to him from the other end. His son, J.P., a United States Naval Academy graduate and Navy lieutenant, had shot and killed his wife's ex-husband.

By midmorning Gene and Carol Kent had secured a lawyer, contacted a pastor near where J.P. was being held, and spoken with their beloved but broken son.

"J.P., we love you and we are here for you," Carol assured him. "We will always love you. You are not alone."

"Thank you, Mom and Dad," was all J.P. could muster.

They prayed over the phone with him for his safety, for his emotional and mental well-being, for the family of his victim, and for God to help them all. Thus began a two-and-a-half-year journey that led to the trial, conviction, and sentencing of their son for first-degree murder.[1]

As extreme as their situation was, Carol and Gene realized that they belonged to a God of extremes. Nothing is too big for Him to handle. Even if all hope of advocacy seems lost, God is at work—in the courtroom, in the prison cell, and in the hearts of all concerned.

> When things go wrong, it's time to regroup and find another way to be an advocate.

There are times when your child's needs may seem to outweigh your ability to advocate for her. Circumstances threaten you like a giant with a club in his hand, while you stand there with only a slingshot and a stone. But God gave you a stone of just the right size, and the aim to shoot it. He provides the tools we need to get the job done—or the power to obey when He asks us to sacrifice our expectations.

For the Kents, the latter was the case. They relied on the promise described in Genesis 22 when the Lord asked Abraham to literally lay down his Isaac as a sacrifice—and then intervened at the last moment. Can we, too, release our grip and let God choose the outcome?

Advocate or Abdicate?

When you hear the word *abdicate*, you may think of a king abdicating his throne. That's a stepping down, like a resignation. When it comes to advocacy, though, abdication is often more temporary. Many of us give up control over decisions that affect our children when we drop them off at the church nursery, the school, the camp, or the laser tag emporium.

We're like builders who assign work to outside contractors. A good builder doesn't walk away from the construction site unless he knows the contractors are doing their jobs. Just as a builder can replace an unsatisfactory contractor, we often can change doctors, teams, schools, and even friends.

But when circumstances seem to rip the parental rights from our hands, or overwhelm our ability to advocate for our kids, we're tempted to make our abdication more permanent.

That kind of resignation is founded on a false belief. We may be convinced that we're not good enough, smart enough, or skilled enough to stand up for our children's needs.

If you're reading this book, you are good enough, smart enough, and capable! Yes, there are people who refuse to parent, but I don't believe that's who you are.

Doctors, lawyers, teachers, coaches, and even relatives aren't the experts on your child. You are. Maybe you don't believe me yet. If so, I challenge you to repeat after me the following call to arms.

> I am my child's best advocate.
> I know him better than anyone else.
> I love him more than any other human ever could.
> I have a higher stake in his future than anyone else does.
> I am the expert on my child. I know him inside and out,
>   for better and for worse.
> I take responsibility for his health, education, and welfare.
> And I will make my stand here and now on his behalf.

Okay—I realize it may take more than that to get you to see who you really are. So let's take the rest of this chapter to deal with some specifics.

Divorce, Custody, and Advocacy

"It's just temporary," John's mother assured him. "Before you know it, Tina will be back and you'll work this out."

John knew better. Tina wasn't coming home, ever. He'd have to get used to the fact that he could no longer tuck his girls into bed each night and read them their favorite bedtime stories—a ritual he felt was one of the many things that had bonded them.

"No, Mom," he said. "Tina's making it impossible for me to be a part of the girls' lives. I know I screwed things up, but that's behind me now. I don't know how to connect with them anymore."

John had fought for equal custody of his three girls, but his state didn't grant that very often. Tina had moved away with their daughters; he had no say in when he might see them again.

"Maybe you should have stay married," his mother said. "This is not good for the kids."

John looked away and laughed—so he wouldn't cry. He couldn't meet his mother's gaze. He knew he'd disappointed her and the rest of his family. But she acted as if it was as easy as saying, "I changed my mind. Let's get back together."

"I wish it was that easy, Mom," he said. "I've already lost so much. Not knowing if Kate needs help with her math, or if Jessie is still seeing that boy, or if Nicole is still not brave enough to face those girls at school who made fun of her that day—it's killing me. I still want to be their hero."

As John found out, any effort to stand up for your children when you're no longer part of your original family unit must adjust to the new "arrangement."

Here are some tips from the experts—and by experts I mean those who've been there and done that.

1. Keep in mind that unless shared parenting is outlined and agreed to, the custodial parent usually maintains the role of primary disciplinarian and nurturer. She or he is the first contact when something goes wrong that requires a parent to step in.

2. When you advocate for your children, leave out negative talk about your ex-spouse's involvement or lack thereof.

3. Work toward healthy communication with your ex-spouse, so that you can meet together any obstacles your children face.

4. Include the other parent in problem solving. Ask sincere questions like, "What do you think we should do?" or "How do you feel about this?"

5. If communicating with the former spouse is especially difficult, consider mediation for the sake of presenting a united front when standing up for your child.

6. Be dependable. Show up on time for meetings related to your child.

7. Be accessible. Make sure your contact information is in the hands of caregivers and service providers. If possible, live close enough that when a situation arises, you can be there in a flash.

8. Parent as a team. The more both parents take part, the more your child will feel connected to each of you.[2]

Each family situation is different. Yours may make joint opportunities for advocacy easier or more difficult. But in light of your calling as a parent, consider doing whatever it takes to promote unity for the sake of your children.

The Noncustodial Parent

Parents without custody can still have a say in their children's lives. It helps, though, to keep the following guidelines in mind.

1. *Know the law governing the rights of noncustodial parents in your state.* If caregivers and service providers exclude you from the decision-making process regarding your child, it may be because they're misinformed. Schools, for instance, may wrongly assume they don't need to contact you if they contact the custodial parent.

Consider doing whatever it takes to promote unity for the sake of your children.

Look for a clause or statute like this one from the Code of Virginia and the Family Educational Rights and Privacy Act: "Notwithstanding any other provision of law, neither parent, regardless of whether such parent has custody, shall be denied access to the academic, medical, hospital or other health records of that parent's minor child unless otherwise ordered by the court for good cause shown." You have the right to know and be involved.

2. *Contact school personnel to make sure you're included as a co-primary contact person for your child.* School officials should consult with both custodial and noncustodial parents on matters involving their children. The assumption should be that both parents have the right to access records unless the school has seen evidence to the contrary.

3. *Remember that with equal rights comes equal responsibility.* If you do arrange shared parenting, make sure that you hold up

your end of the agreement. Be available, respectful, interested, and visible.

4. *Don't vilify the custodial parent.* Even if your divorce wasn't amicable, your ability to advocate for your child will be severely damaged if you malign his or her primary caregiver. Restraining yourself may be uncomfortable, but remember that it's usually best for your child and God's glory.

The Newly Single Parent

The pain of divorce is compounded by your child's pain. Schoolwork and relationships may suffer. Behavior may take a turn for the worse. You may discover that your child engages in self-destructive or dangerous pursuits.

"I find that advocating for my child now is harder just because my ex-husband feels like he can go against me now that we're divorced," one mom observes. "I have an older son who was 16 when my husband left, and he immediately started using drugs. I have so much difficulty with him in and out of juvenile hall—and now that he's 19, he's in jail. Since the divorce, I've advocated for my children alone."

Michelle Campbell, director of women's ministries at Northside Christian Church in Clovis, California, has this advice for parents in that situation: "It's so important to have a strong support team. Friends, church, parents, counselors, can all offer a thick covering of prayer. Single parents are so vulnerable to just being too worn out to fight these battles along with the spiritual, emotional battles of divorce, and all the baggage that goes with it."

As desirable as shared parenting may be, it isn't likely if both parties aren't willing. If you find yourself as lone advocate for your children, Michelle recommends the following:

1. *Pray, pray, pray.* Don't underestimate the power of prayer. You have an advocate in Jesus Christ; make your requests known to Him.

2. *Assemble a strong support team.* Its members should be people who love you unconditionally—preferably including some who know what your life is like because they've survived similar circumstances.

3. *Don't date.* Ron L. Deal, licensed marriage and family therapist and pastor, as well as author of *The Smart Step-Family* (Bethany, 2006), recommends waiting two to three years after divorce before seriously dating. Your children must have top priority during that time; their needs for advocacy can swell to grand proportions, and it's important to focus on them.

4. *Pray some more.*

The Newly Blended Family

According to Maxine Marsolini, author of *Blended Families* (Moody Publishers, 2000) and *Raising Children in Blended Families* (Kregel Publications, 2006), finding ways to balance the needs and concerns of stepparents and stepchildren is a chronic, if not constant, issue. In an interview for this book, Maxine shared her passionate concern for newly blended families when it comes to advocacy:

> Making sure our children's needs are met and feeling confident that appropriate answers to pressing problems can be negotiated is a matter of deep concern for every family. It is my experience that protecting the children not only weighs heavily on the biological parent, but quite often on the step-

parent, too. By entering into a marital relationship with you, this person also agreed to have an active role with your child. But does he or she really have a voice in the matter? A lot will depend on the legal documents governing the divorce. Who has primary custody? Is it joint custody? There isn't a simple solution when it comes to advocating on behalf of children living in stepfamilies. Greater challenges exist.

Unless parental rights have been severed, or a restraining order is in place, there is no question that a biological parent has legal authority to make decisions, get information, and step in the gap on behalf of their children should a medical, educational, or travel situation arise. On the other hand, most stepparents discover their hands are tied. They have a physical presence in the home but no legal relationship between them and their stepchild from which to advocate. This is frustrating. Worse yet, precious time can be wasted when help is needed quickly.

It is advantageous to plan ahead where children are concerned. Consider these suggestions:

- Talk about stepparent authority with your spouse.
- Don't become defensive.
- Listen to each other.
- Be considerate as you take the subject of stepparent authority up with your child's other parent (your ex).
- Do not exhibit an attitude that takes over a birth parent's authority. This is a time when good co-parenting skills work best. You want to create teamwork, not a tug-of-war.
- Keep emotions at bay; remember that protecting the children is the real issue.

- Discuss how much authority is necessary for you, as a stepparent, to have in order to place a safety net around the children. One quick fix is for both custodial parents, or for a biological parent who sees their children some of the time, to sign consent forms with the school or doctor's office giving the stepparent a right to advocate on behalf of their children.

For instance, the stepparent would be able to take your son or daughter to the doctor for stitches after a fall from his or her bicycle. A stepparent could access important information about grades and discipline issues at school should the need arise. By planning ahead, everyone feels more secure—especially the child, knowing a caring adult is ready and able to step in with proper authority. Make it a priority to succeed at advocating well for the sake of your children and the unity of your marriage.

The Parenting Grandparent

Sal was thrilled when his youngest son finally decided to start a family. Sal hadn't found much to care about since his own wife died; having a new granddaughter within arm's reach gave him a renewed sense of life and love.

He looked forward to any and all opportunities to be with this little one. He got that chance more often than planned, though, when his son asked him to babysit regularly while his wife worked. Before he knew it, Sal was parenting his granddaughter much of the time.

Grandparents who parent are hardly unusual these days.

The U.S. Census Bureau reports that more than 3.4 million children are raised by grandparents or other relatives; more than 44 percent of U.S. grandparents spend 100 or more hours per year caring for their grandkids.

Three types of parenting grandparents have been identified: day-care grandparents, "living with" grandparents, and custodial grandparents.

Sal is a day-care grandparent. He's had to adjust his attitude and schedule by putting his granddaughter's needs first. He's purchased toys, equipment, and food to keep in his small apartment in preparation for her visits.

Sal struggles with this arrangement, especially when he thinks his granddaughter isn't getting what she needs. He has concerns over the way she's raised in her own home. He disagrees with the way she's fed (not often enough), when she sleeps (hardly ever), and where she sleeps (in bed with her parents). He's concerned about his daughter-in-law's "forgetfulness" when she says, "I don't remember when I fed her last."

Sal is very protective of this little one. But when it comes to standing up for her, he doesn't know where he stands.

Problems often arise when a grandparent takes on a parental role. Without a specific plan spelling out who's responsible for what, things can get tiresome and tension filled.

If you find yourself caring for your grandchildren, or have enlisted the help of one or both of your parents to care for your children, protect this relationship so that both generations are in a position to stand up for the kids. Here are suggestions:

- Remember that when grandparents help with their grandchildren, their goal should be to support their adult children—not replace them.

- Do what you can to ensure that you and your children (or you and your parents) share the same values, or at least that the values passed along to the child don't contradict each other.
- Don't expect to grandparent in the same way that you parented. You've probably grown and learned much since your own parenting days.
- Lovingly approach one another when there's a difference of opinion on how to handle an issue involving the grandchildren.
- As Arthur Kornhaber, author of *Grandparent Power!* (Three Rivers Press, 1995) puts it, "Be direct and open with your feelings. Roundabout communication accomplishes nothing, and it only allows anger, frustration and disappointment to ferment."[3]

If you're a grandparent, you can advocate for your grandchildren's needs even if you're not involved in their day-to-day care—by standing up for kids in general. Here are a few ideas:

- Keep up with education news in your local paper. Staying informed keeps you abreast of what your grandchildren might be going through.
- Volunteer as a tutor or mentor. Many children don't have grandparents nearby, and you can be the lasting influence they need.
- Evaluate your elected officials' track records of working for better schools.
- Don't stop supporting schools just because you no longer have school-age children. If all grandparents worked for better education, everyone's grandchildren would be taken care of.

"All I Can Do Is Pray for Them"

Remember Diane from the beginning of the chapter? Now that she's relinquished her parental rights, does she have any hope of standing up for her children?

She sees her children now only by virtue of a court order. They don't live in the same state, and Diane doesn't drive. To be with them, she has to take two buses for two hours each way.

She shows up for special occasions like holidays, birthdays, and school plays. But she's not involved in their everyday care and concerns. When something goes wrong at school, which often happens, she doesn't find out about it until weeks later.

"I know my daughter, and I know what works best for her at school," she says. "But I never find out until it's too late that she's having a problem. I don't get to see report cards, or get invited to parent-teacher conferences. I'm not even a contact person on the emergency card. As much as I know that living with me full-time isn't the best idea, there are some areas that I can help with."

> If you're close enough to your child to stand up for him in person, thank God for the privilege.

Diane has tried to get the courts to amend her custody arrangement, but without success. Her kids know that she loves them, but rarely can she stand up for them in person.

"Now all I can do is pray for them," she says. "Interesting, don't you think? That's all my mom could finally do for me."

If praying is the only way you can stand up for your child, be assured that it's not just a last-ditch effort. It's powerful because God is powerful.

If you're close enough to your child to stand up for him in person, prayer should be a top priority, too. When you pray, don't forget to thank God for the privilege of being a visible, hands-on advocate for your child.

Time to Take a Stand

It's been said that parenting is the hardest job you'll ever love. For those of us with a relationship to God, parenting isn't just a job—it's a vocation, a holy calling.

Whether you entered the parenting arena deliberately or were dragged in kicking and screaming, you probably find yourself questioning your ability to stand up for your kids. When that happens, put in your earplugs and put on your blinders so that you can focus on what's true.

The certainty of your calling shouldn't be confused with *feeling* certain. Feelings have nothing to do with it, and tend to gum up the works anyway. No matter how closely you're involved with your children, you can be effective only if you walk with confidence and walk worthy of your calling.

God equips those He calls. He puts in our path the resources we need. He's given us His Word for admonition, encouragement, and instruction, and surrounded us with fellow sojourners to rely on for help. The willingness is up to us.

I can't guarantee that no one will ever be annoyed, frustrated, or even alienated because of your efforts to stand up for your child. But I do know that if you adhere to the guiding principles set forth in this book, you'll become an advocate without being an adversary. It's a delicate balance that takes time, thought—and a commitment to both your child and to God.

NOTES

Chapter 3
1. Adapted from J. Keith Murnighan, *The Dynamics of Bargaining Games* (Upper Saddle River, N.J.: Prentice Hall, 1991), pp. 11-12.

Chapter 4
1. Kerry Patterson et al., *Crucial Confrontations* (New York: McGraw-Hill Books, 2005), p. 93.

Chapter 5
1. Shannon Colavecchio-Van Sickler, "But Professor, My Daughter Deserves an A!" *St. Petersburg Times*, June 19, 2006.

Chapter 7
1. Found at www.prematurity.org/roles.html.

Chapter 8
1. Dr. Reamonn O'Donnchadha, *Eisteach* magazine, found at www.theblackdog.net/fearcruaidh.htm.
2. Adapted from principles contained in George Robert Bach and Peter Wyden, *The Intimate Enemy: How to Fight Fair in Love and Marriage* (New York: Avon Books, 1970).

Chapter 10

1. Carol Kent, *When I Lay My Isaac Down* (Colorado Springs: NavPress, 2004), p. 21.

2. Points 4-8 adapted from Kay Adkins, *I'm Not Your Kid: A Christian's Guide to a Healthy Stepfamily* (Grand Rapids, Mich.: Baker Books, 2004), as excerpted in "Seven Beattitudes for Successful Co-parenting," found at www.successfulstepfamilies.com.

3. Arthur Kornhaber, *Grandparent Power!* (New York: Three Rivers Press, 1995), quoted in Patricia J. Lesesne, "What Grandparents Can Bring to Their Grandchildren and Their Parents," found at www.parenthood.com/articles.html?article_id=7564&printable=true.

Note: Listing of Web sites does not constitute blanket endorsement or complete agreement by Focus on the Family with information or resources offered at or through those sites.

ABOUT THE AUTHOR

Vicki Caruana is, first and foremost, the wife of Chip and the mother of Christopher and Charles. An educator who's taught students in grades from kindergarten through college, she also homeschooled her two children through the elementary years and helped them with their transition into public schools.

Like you, Vicki has found herself standing up for her kids more often than she'd like. She continues to learn how it's done from the greatest model we could have for an advocate, our Lord Jesus Christ.

Vicki's books include the best-selling *Apples & Chalkdust* and *Before the Bell Rings*, as well as *Brain Food: Recipes for Success in School, Sports, and Life* (Rowman & Littlefield, 2007). She has written more than 20 books designed to educate and encourage parents and teachers to strive for excellence.

The author of more than 150 magazine and newspaper articles, Vicki has been a regular contributor to publications such as *Focus on the Family*, *Teachers of Vision*, *Today's Christian Woman*, *Christian Parenting Today*, *The Old Schoolhouse*, *Teach*, PTA's *Our Children*, and many more. She speaks regularly to education, homeschooling, parents', and women's groups about issues surrounding children and education. Vicki is represented by Speak Up Speaker Services; to find out more about including her at your local, regional, national, or international event, contact www.speakupspeakerservices.com.

Vicki is one of four parenting experts to appear on the Focus on the Family DVD *Starting Points*. A regular guest on various

Focus on the Family broadcasts, she is also a contributor to focusonyourchild.com, offering advice on topics such as school choice, goal-setting with kids, giving children the excellence edge, and learning styles.

Born and raised in Staten Island, New York, Vicki lives with her family in Florida, where she teaches at a public middle school. She works with students who have the greatest needs, and is often their only advocate.

Vicki knows what your busy parenting life is like. For more information on her many educational and parenting endeavors, visit her on the Web at www.vickicaruana.blogspot.com and www.standingupforyourchild.blogspot.com.

FREE Discussion Guide!
A reproducible version of this book's discussion questions is available at:

FOCUS ^{ON}_{THE} FAMILY®

Welcome to the family!

Whether you purchased this book, borrowed it, or received it as a gift, we're glad you're reading it. It's just one of the many helpful, encouraging, and biblically based resources produced by Focus on the Family for people in all stages of life.

Focus began in 1977 with the vision of one man, Dr. James Dobson, a licensed psychologist and author of numerous best-selling books on marriage, parenting, and family. Alarmed by the societal, political, and economic pressures that were threatening the existence of the American family, Dr. Dobson founded Focus on the Family with one employee and a once-a-week radio broadcast aired on 36 stations.

Now an international organization reaching millions of people daily, Focus on the Family is dedicated to preserving values and strengthening and encouraging families through the life-changing message of Jesus Christ.

Focus on the Family Magazines

These faith-building, character-developing publications address the interests, issues, concerns, and challenges faced by every member of your family from preschool through the senior years.

| Focus on the Family **Citizen®** U.S. news issues | Focus on the Family **Clubhouse Jr.™** Ages 4 to 8 | Focus on the Family **Clubhouse™** Ages 8 to 12 | **Breakaway®** Teen guys | **Brio®** Teen girls 12 to 16 | **Brio & Beyond®** Teen girls 16 to 19 | **Plugged In®** Reviews movies, music, TV |

FOR MORE INFORMATION

 Online:
Log on to www.family.org
In Canada, log on to www.focusonthefamily.ca

 Phone:
Call toll free: (800) A-FAMILY (232-6459)
In Canada, call toll free: (800) 661-9800

More Great Resources
from Focus on the Family®

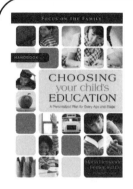

Handbook on Choosing Your Child's Education

Parents today are faced with a wide, often bewildering variety of choices for educating their children, from traditional public schools to private schools, from Christian schools to homeschooling. Focus on the Family's *Handbook on Choosing Your Child's Education* will help parents navigate through the many options and based on their needs, make the best education decision for their children.

20 (Surprisingly Simple) Rules and Tools for a Great Family
by Dr. Steve Stephens

Creating a great family doesn't have to be difficult or require a lot of hard work. It's really about little changes that produce big results. *20 (Surprisingly Simple) Rules and Tools for a Great Family* includes easy-to-apply principles and tools anyone can use to build closer relationships and create lasting memories.

Light from Lucas
by Bob Vander Plaats

The third of four children, Lucas was severely disabled at birth. Through the silent instruction of Lucas, the author and his family relate dozens of lessons they've learned—from knowing God and discovering the value of every life, to practical ideas on parenting and why we suffer.

FOR MORE INFORMATION

 Online:
Log on to www.family.org
In Canada, log on to www.focusonthefamily.ca.

 Phone:
Call toll free: (800) A-FAMILY
In Canada, call toll free: (800) 661-9800.